WOMEN'S SUCCESS IN CORPORATE LEADERSHIP

A GUIDE TO MASTER INFLUENCE, ADVOCACY, INSPIRATION, AND INNOVATION IN BUSINESS FOR A FUTURE PROOFED CAREER NOW

RENÉ CLAYTON

CONTENTS

BOOK OVERVIEW

The book *Women's Success in Corporate Leadership*, is a shining example of inspiration for empowerment. It is a comprehensive guide designed to equip ambitious women with the tools they need to tap into their inner strength, make significant strides in their professional journey, and fortify their careers for the long haul.

Do you want to establish yourself even more as a successful woman in the business world? This book is tailored for you. It provides knowledge, practical advice, and genuine truths essential for transcending societal expectations and achieving remarkable success in today's intensely competitive environment.

Women's Success in Corporate Leadership is more than a book. It is a roadmap that details the subtle nuances you will encounter. Using insightful, real-world examples, it speaks directly to women's challenges and how to rise above them. It offers valuable strategies for personal growth and professional development. Readers will learn why resiliency, self-assurance, and fortitude in the face of the most difficult challenges are not out of reach. As they discover how to embrace and capitalize on those unique traits, women will feel empowered in many aspects of their lives.

In a world where females are occasionally underestimated, *Women's Success in Corporate Leadership* is a waypoint for those who want to change how people view and value them as they climb the rungs of their corporate ladders, determined to make their mark.

INTRODUCTION

You're about to dive into a journey that's not just about soaring to the top of the leadership ladder but transforming how we think about how we lead. The landscape is shifting, and it's exhilarating. Gone are the days when it was a cut-and-dry method, primarily tailored for and by men. Today, the corporate world is waking up to the incredible value women bring to the table—with our diverse viewpoints, strength, vision, resilience, and empathy.

Why this particular guide? Well, it's pretty simple. Throughout my two-decade adventure across the tech and leadership terrains, I've gathered a treasure trove of insights, strategies, and real-world advice I wish someone had shared with me when I stepped into new roles. This book is my way of passing the torch to you, helping you navigate the complex but rewarding journey of shaping leadership in the corporate world.

Resilience lies at the heart of this guide. I assure you that resilience is your very best superpower. It enables us to bounce back from setbacks, draw lessons from them, and strengthen our resolve. It has made it possible for me and many other women to succeed in settings that weren't necessarily made with us in mind.

This book, at its core, is not about women taking the one-way path to leadership, not fitting into the old paradigms, but creating new ones that don't just reflect women's strengths, values, and vision; this is a guide shaped around those. The ones who strive to become a new leader, the ones who have recently been promoted to stars of their team, the team manager, the woman executive trailblazing her path across occasionally intimidating territory, and every woman who is moved by her desire for professional mastery as she stitches it into her life's plan. This book is stacked with pragmatic guidance, inspiring stories, and exquisitely sculpted approaches to accommodate the mysteries and opportunities women face in leadership positions, particularly inside all types of corporations.

While the suggestions in the book are not earth-shattering new, they are the concepts I believe will help you the most. I did leave out parts that other books often discuss, as I did not feel they were relevant to my career path. People have frequently asked me, "How did you get to where you are?" This book is a gift to you to share the ideas and processes that continue to assist me.

What lies ahead on the journey? In this collaborative effort, we shall delve into the realms of advocacy and mentorship, devise strategies for constructing and capitalizing on one's network amidst the dynamic global economy, and uncover the art of authentic leadership that inspires transformative progress. We shall explore methodologies for cultivating resilience, nurturing inclusive teams, and attaining excellence while preserving one's true identity. It is now opportune to retrieve those notebooks and markers and jot down your strategy for becoming the leader you have always aspired to be.

You're not just reading a book; you're stepping into a community of women leaders ready to support, challenge, and inspire one another. Let's get started! The path from entry to excellence is ahead and is ours to shape.

CHAPTER 1
FOUNDATIONS OF FEMALE LEADERSHIP— UNLOCKING YOUR LIGHT

"Do not follow where the path may lead. Go instead where there is no path and leave a trail."

MURIEL STRODE (POET, 1906)

In a busy café, amidst the clinking of coffee cups and the murmur of conversations, a group of diverse individuals gathers around a table. They're not just there for the espresso; they're engaged in a spirited discussion about leadership. This scene, commonplace yet profound, represents a shift in the corporate world that's as refreshing as the aroma of freshly brewed coffee. It's a change from the solitary figure of the autocratic leader to a tapestry of voices, each contributing to a collective vision. This transformation is about altering styles and redefining what it means to lead in today's rapidly changing world.

1.1 REDEFINING LEADERSHIP NOW

The Shift From Autocratic to Collaborative Leadership

Think about the past when leadership was just a one-man show, often without anyone having any additional input. At its core, this was autocratic leadership. It was all about power and making decisions with little input from others. Certainly, it may have accomplished what it set out to do, but it might not have been the most fun or creative method of managing work.

The days of having a single captain and a chain of command have long since passed. Leadership formerly meant command and control. Today's tale is changing to emphasize real teamwork more than ever. This development reflects widespread cultural trends favoring community, communication, and shared goals in various areas of life. Collaborative leadership allows ideas to flow freely by celebrating diverse perspectives and promoting creativity.

This shift is significant for women stepping into leadership roles or expanding their current positions. Why? Many women naturally shine in the qualities that make collaborative leadership work—like being a great listener, showing empathy, creating visibility, and bringing people together. We generate amazing ideas when everyone contributes their ideas!

By moving towards a more combined approach, we're not just making the workplace better for women; we're making it better for everyone. It's about building spaces where each person's ideas are heard and valued, leading to more well-rounded and happier teams. We all need leaders we can aspire to emulate and learn from. That is, you!

Throughout the world, trust is the currency of leadership. As a result, we shape our own destiny, employing courage to create a legacy by actively seeking out exceptional qualities in everyday life; we possess the wisdom to recognize every challenge as a potential opportunity.

In summary, as our time at the café scene suggests, leadership today is not a monologue but a chorus. It's a dynamic interplay of all types of voices, each with its own timbre and pitch, coming together to create a harmony that resonates with innovation, empathy, connection, and inclusivity. The shift from autocratic to collaborative leadership, the rise of emotional intelligence, and the impact of diversity with inclusion are not just trends; they are signposts pointing towards a more vibrant, equitable, and organic future for leadership. Let us now dive deeper.

1.2 THE POWER OF AUTHENTIC LEADERSHIP

Understandably, standing out can seem like a gamble in a world that often values conformity. However, female leaders who stay true to themselves and stick with their principles stand out from the crowd and motivate those around them. Genuine leadership is not just about being honest; it entails maintaining commitment to one's values, accountability for one's actions, and frankness in all communication. This type of leadership makes people happier and helps the group succeed.

Think of it this way: Authentic leadership is akin to being the protagonist of your favorite book. I love to read books with engaging and genuine main characters. You're not acting when you lead; you are just being who you are, with all your faults and all. This means showing up genuinely as yourself and relating to your team members in a real and vulnerable manner. Acting out fictitious roles while on the clock is not the limit of this leadership style; it's about being genuine and encouraging others to do the same.

That is why this message can often resonate more deeply with women than with men. In most cases, we have found ourselves trying to fit into predefined molds, attempting to lead in a certain way, or copying styles that do not precisely match our personalities. But there is a catch: characteristics such as resilience, empathy, intuition, and adaptability—traditionally undervalued in many professional settings—have emerged as compelling leadership qualities, particularly in the face of global challenges and changing work environments. This shift represents a significant opportunity for women, who often inherently possess or have honed these traits through navigating societal expectations and personal challenges. It signifies the recognition of previously overlooked or dismissed attributes as critical for effective leadership and career growth.

Moreover, this shift benefits not just females but all leaders. Different leadership styles and viewpoints result in more creative approaches, improved team behavior, and an inclusive work environment. When companies value our contributions, we can unleash new levels of creativity.

What's the honest power of authentic leadership? It's about breaking down the barriers, ditching the "shoulds," and leading with our true selves. It's about creating spaces where everyone feels valued and heard and where authenticity is the gold standard.

We can lead more successfully by embracing our true selves and creating a new benchmark for inclusive, sincere, and profoundly influential leadership.

Defining Your Leadership Approach

In the world of leadership, where each complicated road is as unique as the person following it, defining your approach to leadership is like locating your north star. It's about creating a personal statement that steers you through calm and turbulent times. The goal here is to shape your journey, not to fit into a box or emulate someone else's.

Think of leadership as a vast ocean. Some are the steadfast lighthouses guiding from afar, and others are the captains steering the ship. How do you "walk and talk?" How do you show up? How are you "with" people? How do you inspire and motivate? Think about this as you embark upon your goals.

Finding out what your leadership approach is takes time. It means discovering yourself through trial and error and accepting your successes and failures. When you realize that being a leader is not just a position but an authentic reflection of who you truly are and that being a leader is not easy, it's tough but worth it, too!

For the women charting their course in leadership, remember this: Your style is your signature and your brand. It's unique, evolving, and irreplaceably yours. By embracing it, you're not just navigating the vast leadership ocean; you're changing its currents and making waves that inspire those who sail with you.

Developing your distinct leadership style is like learning to speak in a crowded room for the first time. It starts with introspection, understanding your strengths, weaknesses, and the values that guide you. Consider a leader who finds strength in calmness and deliberation. For them, leadership might mean creating spaces for reflection and thoughtful decision-making within their team. On the other hand, a leader with a natural inclination towards enthusiasm and motivation might focus on energizing their team, driving them towards goals with passion and energy.

1.3 9 CRITICAL PROCESSES TO DEFINE AND REFINE YOUR LEADERSHIP

The journey towards attaining leadership status is inherently personal and requires ongoing self-reflection and adaptation; it does not adhere to a standard formula. Recognizing and enhancing one's approach has become more critical in a constantly evolving world. A deliberate undertaking involving introspection, input gathering, and education is necessary to harmonize one's personal values, strengths, and aspirations with one's team and the organization's overarching goals. Leaders who possess a solid understanding of essential leadership principles, exhibit receptiveness to diverse perspectives, and proactively strive for personal growth and flexibility in response to evolving conditions create an exemplary precedent that inspires others to emulate and accomplish remarkable feats. Developing a distinctive leadership approach is a continuous endeavor that will yield substantial benefits in the workplace and in personal life. In the book, we will dive deeper into the nine areas below:

The 9 Processes

1. Understand the Core Leadership Approach

- Familiarize yourself with the primary leadership styles and approaches—autocratic, democratic, transformational, transactional, servant, and situational leadership. Each has its own context, advantages, and drawbacks. Knowing these can help you identify which one(s) align with your personality, values, and organizational needs.

2. Self-Assessment and Reflection

- Reflect on your values, strengths, weaknesses, and the impact you want to have as a leader. Tools like CliftonStrengths can provide insights into your behavioral tendencies and how they align with leadership styles.

3. Testing

- Experiment with various leadership styles rather than settling for the best one.

4. Adaptability

- The most effective leaders can adapt their style to their team's needs and the situation's demands. Understanding situational leadership is crucial to adjusting your approach based on the task, the team's capabilities, and the environment.

5. Feedback and Growth

- Regular feedback from peers, mentors, and team members is invaluable for developing your leadership style. It helps identify areas for improvement and confirms what aspects of your leadership are most helpful.

6. Vision and Communication

- Regardless of the style, influential leaders are visionaries who clearly and compellingly articulate their vision to others. They inspire and motivate their team towards achieving common goals. Developing strong communication skills is essential to becoming an effective leader.

7. Empathy with Emotional Intelligence

- A significant part of leadership involves understanding and managing your emotions and those of your team members. Leaders with high emotional intelligence can build stronger relationships, foster a positive work environment, and navigate conflicts more effectively. We will dive deeper into this topic in a later chapter.

8. Show the Way

- Your actions set the tone for your team's behavior and work ethic. Practicing what you preach and demonstrating the values you want your team to embody are essential for being a good leader.

9. Never Stop Learning

- The best leaders are perpetual learners. Stay informed about new leadership theories, industry trends, technology, and the broader world. This constant learning helps you stay up-to-date and creative.

Focusing on these nine areas will help you clearly define your approach and understand how to utilize it successfully in your position. Remember, leadership is not the same for everyone; it's about finding the approach that resonates with you and meets the needs of those you lead.

Being true to yourself and exhibiting transparency, integrity, and a strong sense of purpose are hallmarks of authentic leadership. It compels us to contemplate our values, identity, and approaches to leadership, ensuring they are authentically in line with our true selves.

Aligning Personal Values With Leadership Goals

Once you have carved out your leadership approach, the next step is to ensure that it aligns with your values and the objectives you aim to achieve. This alignment is what gives your leadership its authenticity and power. It's about making decisions that drive progress and resonate with your core beliefs. For instance, if integrity is one of your fundamental values, your leadership should reflect this through transparent decision-making processes, even when it may be easier to take shortcuts.

Your values are your compass, guiding your decisions, actions, and interactions. They are the silent whispers of your heart, shaping your beliefs and view of the world. These values are uniquely yours, whether it's integrity, compassion, or courage. Recognizing and honoring these values is the first step toward authentic leadership. When your actions as a leader reflect your true self, you gain respect and inspire those around you to follow suit.

The journey to alignment begins with self-reflection. Ask yourself: What matters most to me? How can my values drive my goals as a leader? This introspection reveals the harmony (or discord) between your inner beliefs and your leadership aspirations. To bridge any gaps, set leadership goals that resonate with your values. Remember, alignment is a continuous process, requiring regular check-ins with yourself to ensure your leadership path remains true to your values.

This unity can make it easier for your team members to trust you. Not only that, but they also see a leader who not only talks the talk but walks the walk, creating a culture of real accountability and ethical behavior. It also guarantees that your leadership goals are not just about achieving targets but about creating a legacy of values you and your group are proud to stand by. Members of your team's performance and loyalty take a nosedive when they feel abandoned, reliant, or neglected. To maximize their participation and dedication, it is crucial to cultivate an atmosphere that gives people agency, promotes independence, and makes them feel like they belong.

Leaders that I have looked up to the most have these qualities, and I have tried to emulate them throughout my career.

Practical Steps

- **Define your core values:** Clearly articulate what values are non-negotiable.
- **Set leadership goals:** Ensure these goals align with your values.
- **Review regularly:** Continuously check that your actions and decisions align and adjust as necessary.

Being Honest and Transparent in Leadership

In the tapestry of authentic leadership, transparency and honesty are the golden threads that hold everything together. They're about more than just telling the truth; they're about being transparent about your thoughts, decisions, and uncertainties. It is about admitting when you are unsure or willing to work with your team to discover solutions.

Transparency fosters a culture of trust. Keeping team members informed increases their engagement and commitment. Sincerity also builds respect. It shows your team that you value them enough to be truthful, even in difficult situations. Transparency creates an environment where open communication is encouraged, and feedback flows freely, leading to more innovative and resilient teams.

How to Accomplish the Task

- **Communicate openly:** Share your thought processes, decisions, and the reasons behind them with your team.
- **Encourage feedback:** Create channels for open and honest feedback, showing that you value your team's input.
- **Admit mistakes:** Quickly own up to mistakes, showing that failure and learning are safe.

Authentic leadership involves embracing your unique style, aligning it with your core values, and leading openly. It's not only practical but also deeply rewarding, both for you and those you lead.

1.4 EMBRACING VULNERABILITY IN LEADERSHIP

Modern leadership now views vulnerability as a powerful strength rather than a weakness. Being vulnerable may appear weak, but being genuine in your work is essential. This idea challenges conventional leadership by encouraging leaders to discuss their doubts and struggles. Being transparent does not diminish a leader's power; it humanizes them and helps build stronger bonds inside their teams and throughout the company.

The Beauty of Failure: Converting Mistakes into Milestones

The fear of failure can often feel like a towering barrier to innovation and risk-taking. Yet, when leaders reframe failure not as a setback but as a critical step toward discovery, they unlock a culture of growth and resilience. This shift begins with leaders openly sharing their missteps and the lessons gleaned from them. Such transparency demystifies the path to success and encourages team members to step out of their comfort zones, knowing that failure is tolerated and valued as a learning tool. None of this may be easy, but I assure you, it will be worth it!

Throughout my career, I have experienced failure. It taught me many lessons about what I could have done better, how to take responsibility, and what I learned from the different situations. In one of my first positions as a program manager, I noticed a potential scheduling conflict but kept quiet. My fear of not appearing collaborative caused me to stay silent. Unfortunately, this led to a significant delay in the project. I learned the hard way about the consequences of being passive and hesitant. Now, I make sure to voice any uncertainties or concerns. Discovering I am wrong is better than letting a minor issue escalate into a serious one.

Failure is not the opposite of success, but a launch pad towards it. Every misstep and setback holds lessons awaiting discovery. Consider treating every failure not as a dead end but as a detour to a better destination. This change in perspective isn't just inspiring; it has a profound impact. It encourages strength, sparks creativity, and promotes a spirit of perseverance that no book or success story can teach.

Acknowledge your mistakes, but more importantly, dissect them. What went wrong? What should we do differently the next time? This reflective process turns painful experiences into insightful lessons. Moreover, sharing your failures and the lessons learned creates a culture of openness and support. It dismantles the stigma around failing, showing that it's not a weakness but a testament to one's courage to try. You learn from your own experiences and pave the way for others to navigate their failures gracefully.

Embracing disappointment liberates us from the fear of making mistakes. It allows us to live fully, try new things, and pursue our goals with a heart full of courage. Remember, every great achiever in history has faced failures, but what set them apart was their willingness to use these experiences as a foundation for growth. Let's celebrate our failures as much as our successes, for they are integral to the beautiful journey of becoming. My motto is to fail fast, learn, and begin again.

Practical Steps

- Share stories of past failures and the lessons learned.
- Celebrate "failures" in team meetings, focusing on the learnings rather than the setbacks.
- Create a "safe-to-fail" project culture, encouraging innovative ideas with the understanding that not all will succeed.
- Encourage risk-taking within reasonable boundaries and view failures as learning opportunities rather than setbacks.
- Fail Fast.

Encouraging Open Dialogue for Innovation

Innovation thrives through communication and feedback in a society where all voices count. Let us start with how establishing a communicative climate can stimulate groundbreaking innovations.

Transparency is integral to a dynamic and innovative team. In this place, various ideas combine to create solutions and strategies that no one could have thought of. In my many years as a corporate executive and manager, nothing could be more valid than this statement. This entails actively listening to team members, acknowledging their input, and responding positively. It is imperative not just to pretend to be listening. The process may be uncomfortable; leaders must set aside their egos, become open-minded about criticisms, and include compassion. As teams discover their power during unguarded conversations, while you are assuming the best, they share objectives and respect each other mutually by working together.

Being an innovative female leader takes this concept to a whole new level, and it is more than just coming up with creative ideas. It entails fostering a supportive atmosphere for creativity, showing empathy, empowering and motivating others to contribute ideas, and effectively implementing them to achieve organizational success. This environment accelerates personal growth and propels projects and ideas forward in previously unimaginable ways. As we embrace these principles, we spur innovation and build stronger, more resilient communities. Let's commit to being architects of this change, one conversation at a time.

Practical Steps

- Hold regular "open floor" meetings where team members can voice ideas and concerns without backlash.
- Implement a feedback system that allows anonymous contributions to ensure everyone feels comfortable sharing.
- Lead by example, actively seeking feedback on your leadership and demonstrating how to accept it constructively.
- Empower team members by providing resources, delegating authority, and offering support. Empowered employees are likely to take initiative, experiment with new approaches, and drive change.
- Diverse teams bring various perspectives, ideas, and experiences, especially in a global setting, which is invaluable for innovation.

Striking a Balance Between Decision-Making and Empathy

Empathy in your position as a leader is more than understanding others' feelings; it's about incorporating this understanding into decision-making processes. It's a delicate balance, requiring leaders to consider the human impact of their decisions while staying aligned with the company's goals. This empathetic approach doesn't mean shying away from tough choices but rather navigating them with care, considering the well-being of team members alongside business outcomes. It's about explaining the why behind decisions, especially the hard ones, so team members feel seen and valued even in challenging times.

On the other hand, people often view decision-making through a prism of logic and analysis. Weighing options, assessing risks, and forecasting outcomes refine this process. However, infusing empathy into this process doesn't dilute its effectiveness; it enhances it. Empathy brings a human-centric perspective to decision-making, ensuring thoughtful and kind choices. It helps navigate the complex emotional landscapes of those affected, making decisions more inclusive and sustainable. Balancing empathy with analytical rigor allows leaders to achieve goals and inspire and uplift.

Striking a balance between empathy and making decisions is no easy feat, as delicate as walking a tightrope. It requires courage to remain open-hearted despite tough choices and discipline to remain clear-headed when emotions run high. The key lies in valuing both aspects equally and understanding that every decision impacts lives. By championing empathy in our decision-making, we craft a leadership style that is both compassionate and effective, paving the way for a culture of empathy-led innovation.

Practical Steps

- Before making significant decisions, consider the potential impact on your team, not just the business unit or company.
- Communicate decisions transparently, sharing the reasoning and acknowledging the human element involved.
- Implement support structures for decisions that might harm the team, showing that while tough choices are necessary, the well-being of team members remains a clear priority.

Leadership changes constantly, and empathy stands out as a thread that runs through the fabric of good teams, holding people together with trust, resiliency, and new ideas. It's a testament to the strength of openness, the growth spurred by failure, and the unity fostered by empathy. Leaders who embrace this trait not only maintain their authority but also strengthen it, fostering teams that not only share a common vision but also bolster each other's respect and under-standing.

1.5 LEADERSHIP AS A JOURNEY, NOT A DESTINATION

When women lead, the idea of a final, triumphant arrival point is a myth. Effective leadership, on the other hand, develops over time through situations, learning, and being open to change. This point of view changes the focus from trying to reach the highest level of success to embracing a road of constant growth and change.

Why Leadership Development Must Be an Ongoing Priority

New challenges and opportunities pop up rapidly in corporate America. Do not remain static. Lifelong career development becomes a favorable habit and a necessary mindset for those aiming to lead with relevance and impact, especially if you want to future-proof your career.

Practical Steps

- **Embracing a Curious Mindset:** Curiosity fuels lifelong learning. It drives leaders to question the status quo, seek new knowledge, and explore unfamiliar territories. This mindset encourages openness to new ideas and perspectives, which supports team innovation and creativity.
- **Continuous Skill Development:** The skills that got you to a leadership position will differ from those that sustain you there. As technology advances and business models evolve, so must a leader's skills. Whether it's deepening your understanding of digital transformation, enhancing your emotional intelligence, or mastering the art of remote team management, the commitment to nonstop skill development ensures you remain an effective leader.
- **Knowledge from Diverse Sources:** Lifelong learning is more than just formal education or training programs. It encompasses various sources, from books and podcasts to conferences and peer networks. Engaging with diverse learning resources enriches your leadership approach with multiple perspectives and insights.

Adapting to Change and Uncertainty

Change is the only constant in today's corporate world, and uncertainty often accompanies it. It challenges our comfort zones and tests our resilience. Women leaders who can navigate this uncertainty with agility and resilience set themselves and their teams up for success. Adaptability in leadership is about more than just reacting to change;

it's about anticipating it, preparing for it, and driving your team confidently through it.

As the future of our professions becomes more obscured, the prospect of navigating it might feel more and more frightening. Our resourcefulness and flexibility shine through in these times of uncertainty. It makes us more adaptable, able to change our course when things get tough, and comfortable with uncertainty. When the road ahead does not appear straight, this reminds us that we have a compass within, which urges us to trust the process and ourselves. To become all we can be, we strip off the shackles of fear in the name of freedom.

Change and uncertainty are delicate arts perfected over time through resilience and practice. This entails having an open heart, a resilient spirit, and a never-dying belief in being able to thrive. This art is about survival and thriving, so every difficulty becomes one step closer to realizing our dreams. Let us embrace change and uncertainty with boldness and curiosity because they are the builders of who we are personally and open doors for our greatest accomplishments.

Applying the Approach

- **Creating a Culture of Agility:** Leaders who embrace change cultivate a culture that values and encourages adaptability. This involves empowering team members to make decisions, encouraging experimentation, and viewing failures as learning opportunities. Such a culture is resilient in the face of change, with individuals ready to pivot strategies and innovate solutions.
- **Strategic Flexibility:** Having a clear vision and strategy is vital, as is the flexibility to adjust them in response to changing circumstances. This doesn't mean being aimless

but being prepared to recalibrate goals and approaches based on new information or emerging trends. Strategic flexibility empowers leaders to seize change's opportunities instead of ignoring them.

- **Emotional Resilience:** Navigating change and uncertainty can be emotionally taxing, not just for leaders but also for their teams. Building emotional resilience involves managing one's reactions to severe stress and awful setbacks, maintaining a positive outlook, and supporting one's team through challenges. Leaders who exhibit these qualities inspire confidence and stability, even in the most turbulent of times.

The Value of Self-Evaluation and Reflection on Leadership Development

Your leadership development toolkit must include reflection and self-assessment as fundamental ingredients. These serve as mirrors through which leaders may scrutinize their actions and decisions and impact others to learn lessons or build upon such experiences.

It is also the pause between action and reaction, a moment to breathe and look back with intent. It allows leaders to sift through their experiences, celebrating successes and understanding missteps. This practice isn't about dwelling on the past but learning from it. By regularly holding a mirror to our actions, we can see who we are and who we can become. This clarity fuels our evolution, guiding us towards more mindful leadership.

Merging reflection and self-assessment into the fabric of your leadership style transforms challenges into opportunities for learning and growth. This integration fosters a leadership approach that is both responsive and responsible, characterized by self-awareness and adaptability. As we journey through the leadership landscape, let these practices guide us, ensuring that we grow as leaders and individuals, ready to inspire change and make a lasting impact.

Key Factors

- **Regular Reflection Practices:** Incorporating regular reflection into your routine allows you to pause, assess your leadership journey, and make necessary adjustments. This could be through journaling, meditation, or structured debriefs after significant projects or events. These practices help crystallize lessons learned, celebrate successes, and identify areas for future development.
- **Seeking and Acting on Feedback:** Feedback offers invaluable insights into your leadership effectiveness from those you lead and work with. Actively seeking feedback through formal reviews, 360-degree evaluations, or informal conversations demonstrates a commitment to self-improvement. More importantly, acting on this feedback shows a dedication to becoming the best leader you can be.
- **Setting Personal Development Goals:** Reflection and self-assessment should culminate in actionable personal and professional growth goals. These goals, rooted in the insights gained from reflection and feedback, guide your learning and development activities. They ensure that your growth as a leader is intentional, focused, and aligned with your aspirations and the needs of your team and organization.

The Influence of Diversity on Leadership Participation

Our concept of successful leadership has evolved over the years. When the range of relevant stories, viewpoints, and relationships in leadership is enlarged, these identities can bring a fuller life to the concepts. In this vein, McKinsey & Company's research highlights the relationship between diversity in leadership and enterprise financial performance. Data shows that companies with diverse executive teams outperformed their less varied peers in profitability and sustainability by a statistically significant margin. These teams are better across the board; they comprehend customer needs and offer novel solutions in difficult situations.

However, diversity and inclusion have implications beyond numbers on a balance sheet. They also define an organization's culture, making it adaptable, fresh, and open. Different backgrounds bring different ways of thinking about challenges and solving them, leading decision-making processes, while leaders emerge from various backgrounds. Moreover, an inclusive leadership model delivers a resounding message concerning the worthiness of everyone within the organization, motivating workers to come up with their best ideas.

Ultimately, the difference between the good and the great is a desire to grow and be open to change. If you see leadership as an ongoing learning process involving adapting, reflecting, and self-evaluation, you will stay relevant and have an effect. The way to becoming a leader is through discovery, where each step forward is a chance to learn, improve, and develop new ideas.

CHAPTER 2
STANDING ON THE SHOULDERS OF GIANTS

"I think the truth is that people who end up as 'first' don't set out to be first. They set out to do something they love. And it just so happens that they are the first to do it."

CONDOLEEZZA RICE (DIPLOMAT, DIRECTOR OF THE HOOVER INSTITUTION AT STANDFORD UNIVERSITY, 2016)

I magine stepping into a space brimming with some of the most impactful female leaders of our time, ready to share their wisdom and insights. The power of learning from those who have paved the way before us, transforming their sectors and, in many cases, the very concept of leadership itself. The stories of these trailblazers are not just tales of personal triumph but blueprints that can guide our paths to leadership excellence.

This chapter highlights three extraordinary women whose leadership styles and achievements have broken glass ceilings and reshaped corporate businesses. Their journeys underscore the importance of vision, transformation, and pioneering in leadership. Through their eyes, we glean practical wisdom and strategies that can inspire our leadership approach, regardless of the stage in our careers.

2.1 BOLD MOVES: INSIGHTS FROM VISIONARY WOMEN LEADERS

In the sphere where leadership intertwines with innovation and courage, many women stand as guiding lights, illuminating paths previously untraveled. These extraordinary leaders have reshaped their industries through bold decisions and laid down the markers for effective, transformative leadership. Their unique perspective and innovative ideas set them apart from the ordinary.

Pioneering Women in Leadership

Across industries, women leaders have often faced the dual challenge of navigating their roles, traditionally dominated by men, while pushing the boundaries of what is expected. Yet, within these challenges lie incredible stories of innovation, resilience, and strategic foresight.

I often think of the women who were mathematicians in the 1950s and, as we know today, computer programmers. When the space programs moved along, they hired diverse women who could provide mathematical skills and data analysis—they were called "human computers." These incredible women made history with their grit and willingness to learn. Let us explore the stories of other remarkable women and their journeys to create the path.

Stories of Women Paving the Way

Technology Innovator

In the tech world, where one thing that never changes is speed, women leaders have spearheaded groundbreaking initiatives, from AI advancements to global e-commerce platforms. Their approach combines cutting-edge technology with a keen understanding of user needs, driving product innovation and user experience enhancements.

Whitney Wolfe Herd, the CEO and founder of Bumble, a dating app that empowers women by allowing only female users to initiate contact with matched male users, is one notable female tech leader making bold moves.

After college, Wolfe Herd co-founded Tinder, where she was vice president of marketing. However, a well-publicized departure involving a sexual harassment lawsuit against the company, settled without admission of wrongdoing, marked the end of her journey with Tinder. This challenging period in her career became a turning point. It led her to ideate a dating platform to give women control over their interactions, fundamentally changing the dating app landscape.

In 2014, Wolfe Herd founded Bumble with the backing of Andrey Andreev, the founder of the dating site Badoo. Since its inception, Bumble has been centered around creating a respectful and empowering online dating environment for women. The app's unique feature—giving women the power to initiate conversations—was revolutionary and addressed the imbalance and often negative experiences women faced in online dating.

Under Wolfe Herd's leadership, Bumble has grown exponentially. It went public in February 2021, making Wolfe Herd the world's youngest self-made female billionaire at the time. Beyond its success as a business, Bumble has been a part of a larger conversation about gender dynamics, online safety, and women's empowerment in the digital age.

Social Changemaker

Beyond the corporate sphere, women have led movements and organizations aimed at addressing some of the most pressing social issues of our time. Through strategic advocacy, community building, and innovative problem-solving, they've brought attention and solutions to matters overlooked, setting new standards for leadership in social change.

In the realm of social change through technology, Dr. Rana el Kaliouby stands out as a pioneering female leader. She is an Egyptian-American computer scientist, entrepreneur, and co-founder and CEO of Affectiva, a company that broke new ground in Emotion AI, a subset of artificial intelligence that enables machines to understand and respond to human emotions. Her work has pushed the boundaries of what AI can achieve and laid the foundation for a more humane and empathetic approach to technology.

Born and raised in Cairo, Egypt, Rana el Kaliouby was deeply influenced by her father, who was a technology enthusiast. She pursued her undergraduate degree in computer science at the American University in Cairo, where she first became fascinated with computers' potential to revolutionize human life. Her passion for technology led her to the University of Cambridge, where she earned her Ph.D. in computer science, specifically in the fields of machine learning and emotion recognition.

During her postdoctoral work at MIT Media Lab, el Kaliouby's research focused on developing algorithms to understand human emotions based on facial expressions and physiological responses. This work was personal for el Kaliouby; she wanted to bridge the communication gap she experienced while communicating with her family in Egypt through digital means, recognizing the vast potential for technology to convey human emotions more effectively.

In 2009, she co-founded Affectiva with Professor Rosalind Picard to commercialize Emotion AI technology. Affectiva's mission was to humanize technology by integrating emotional intelligence into digital interactions, making machines more responsive to human states and emotions. This technology has wide-ranging applications, from enhancing customer experience and automotive safety to mental health support and educational tools.

El Kaliouby's work has received widespread recognition for its innovative blending of emotional intelligence with artificial intelligence. She has been featured in Forbes' Top 50 Women in Tech and named one of Fortune's 40 Under 40. Her book, "Girl Decoded," chronicles her journey from a young girl in Cairo to a prominent tech CEO in the United States, highlighting the personal and professional challenges she overcame and her vision for a technology-enhanced future that understands and respects human emotions.

Under her leadership, Affectiva has become a leading player in Emotion AI, influencing how businesses and developers conceive of and integrate AI into products requiring a nuanced understanding of human emotions. Her advocacy for ethical AI development and application underscores her commitment to using technology as a force for good, ensuring that advancements in AI contribute positively to society.

Industry Trailblazer

From finance to manufacturing, women at the helm have often had to rewrite the rules, introducing new models of leadership that emphasize collaboration, sustainability, and ethical practices. Their leadership styles frequently reflect a blend of solid vision, inclusivity, and a commitment to long-term, impactful change, challenging the status quo and setting new benchmarks for industry practices.

In the financial industry, historically dominated by male leadership, Jane Fraser stands out as a trailblazing female leader. As the CEO of Citigroup, she marked a significant milestone by becoming the first woman to lead a major Wall Street bank. Jane is now part of the 100 Most Influential Women in U.S. Finance in 2024. Fraser's ascent to this role is a personal achievement and a watershed moment for gender diversity in the finance sector, signaling progress in breaking the industry's glass ceiling.

Born in Scotland, Jane Fraser's academic background is as impressive as her professional trajectory. She holds an M.B.A. from Harvard Business School and a Master of Arts in economics from Cambridge University. Early in her career, Fraser honed her global perspective, which has been instrumental in navigating the complex international operations of a banking giant like Citigroup.

Fraser's leadership comes at a critical time for the banking industry, facing challenges from digital transformation, regulatory pressures, and the need for sustainable practices. Her approach has been characterized by a commitment to leveraging technology to enhance banking services, prioritizing customer experience, and advocating for environmental sustainability and diversity within the bank's operations and leadership. Under her leadership, Citigroup announced its commitment to achieving net-zero greenhouse gas emissions by 2050, reflecting the growing trend of integrating sustainability into corporate strategy.

Jane Fraser's impact extends beyond Citigroup's operational success. Her leadership is dismantling long-standing gender stereotypes in finance, inspiring a new generation of women to aspire to leadership positions in the industry. She has been vocal about the challenges women face in the workplace, including work-life balance and the need for more supportive corporate cultures that enable women to pursue career and family life without sacrificing one for the other.

Jane Fraser's story is emblematic of the gradual but determined shift towards more inclusive and diverse leadership in the financial sector. Her achievements underscore the importance of perseverance, expertise, and the willingness to challenge the status quo. As the financial industry continues to evolve, Fraser's role as a leader and a pioneer will undoubtedly influence the direction of Citigroup and the broader conversation about women in leadership positions within the global financial landscape (Moyer, 2024).

2.2 LESSONS FROM THEIR BOLD MOVES

Examining the trajectories of these visionary leaders, several vital lessons emerge that apply to anyone aiming to lead with impact in today's complex world.

- **Embrace Risk with Strategic Intent:** These leaders have repeatedly shown that calculated risks, backed by thorough research and strategic planning, can lead to significant breakthroughs. Their journeys underscore the importance of not shying away from bold decisions but embracing them as opportunities for growth and innovation.
- **Foster Inclusivity at Every Level:** Their leadership approach emphasizes the creation of inclusive environments that not only hear diverse voices but also integrate them into decision-making processes. This commitment to

inclusivity has often been a driving force behind their ability to innovate and adapt.

- **Sustain Your Vision with Tenacity:** Their leadership is characterized by their persistent approach to overcoming challenges. They demonstrate that sustaining your vision, even when faced with setbacks, is crucial to driving long-term change. Their stories highlight the power of resilience and the importance of staying true to your core values and objectives.

2.3 THE IMPACT OF THEIR LEADERSHIP

The influence of these pioneering women extends far beyond their immediate industries or sectors. They have achieved remarkable success in their fields and catalyzed broader cultural and societal shifts in perceptions of leadership.

- **Redefining Leadership Paradigms:** By leading with a blend of creativity, acceptance, and strength, they have challenged and expanded traditional notions of leadership. Their success is a powerful counter-narrative to prevailing stereotypes, inspiring a new generation of leaders across genders and industries.
- **Driving Systemic Change:** The impact of their leadership is evident in the systemic changes they've championed, from transforming business models to advocating for policy reforms. Their bold moves have often catalyzed broader shifts, influencing practices, standards, and norms within their spheres of influence.
- **Cultivating a Legacy of Empowerment:** Perhaps most importantly, their leadership journeys have paved the way for future generations, creating pathways and possibilities where there were none. Through mentorship, advocacy,

and example, they have empowered others to pursue
leadership roles, fostering a culture of opportunity, growth,
and change.

Through their eyes, we see the leadership landscape as a canvas of opportunity where our unique strengths and visions can leave indelible marks. By applying the lessons from their experiences, we equip ourselves with the tools to navigate our leadership paths with confidence and purpose. Reflecting on their stories reminds us of the profound impact thoughtful, inclusive, and visionary leadership can have on our organizations and the world.

CHAPTER 3
INFLUENCE AND ADVOCACY

"Leadership is about making others better as a result of your presence and making sure that impact lasts in your absence."

SHERYL SANDBERG (PRIOR COO OF FACEBOOK, 2013)

Recall when you went to a lively networking event, weaving in and out of people as you said hello. Suddenly, you find yourself drawn to a corner of the room where a woman speaks. It's not just her words that captivate you, but her presence, confidence, and way of making everyone around her feel seen and heard. She speaks, and the room listens, not out of obligation but because they genuinely want to. This, right here, is influence in action. It's not about titles or authority but inspiring others to listen, engage, and act.

Women in business gracefully and intentionally navigate traditional expectations and contemporary desires. They represent the transforming power of inclusive leadership, which fundamentally thrives on divergent views, empathy, and collective effort. Their leadership style is based on understanding, emotional intelligence, and the willingness to experience pain, as opposed to the outdated paradigm that values assertiveness and control. This does not diminish but enriches their firmness of purpose, implying that their influence is not just about position but a proof of character.

A woman often encounters a maze of prejudices and obstacles during her journey through the business world. Thus, their influence finds its most profound expression within these complexities. By passing through such challenges, women leaders become models for stamina and fortitude, guiding others along similar paths. They extend their impact beyond the boardrooms and deep into corporate culture to stitch a more inclusive, compassionate fabric.

The influence of women in leadership extends beyond organizational boundaries. It's about creating ripples that turn into waves, reshaping corporate cultures and industry standards. Women leaders are not just filling seats; they're redefining what it means to lead. Their methodology frequently incorporates emotional intelligence, teamwork, and a comprehensive view of success—elements that lead to more enduring and inclusive advancement.

Evidence suggests that companies with more women in leadership positions tend to perform better in profitability, creativity, and employee satisfaction. This is not about pitting genders or races against each other but about highlighting the value of diversity in driving organizational success.

In the corporate world, where decisions are made, projects are initiated, and change is a constant, influence is a cornerstone of effective leadership. It's about impact, driving results, and guiding teams toward shared goals. But how does one build this kind of influence? Let's explore the essentials: trust, credibility, persuasive communication, and the often-overlooked role of emotional intelligence.

3.1 3 KEYS TO YOUR IMPACT

Key 1: Building Trust and Credibility

Trust and credibility are essential for constructing relationships in leadership architecture that stand the test of time. Let's explore how we can nurture and maintain these foundational elements to ensure a leadership legacy that resonates with integrity and authenticity.

Trust is the foundation of any strong connection, be it personal or professional. Reliability, consistently showing up, and delivering on promises are the cornerstones of building trust. Being honest about your goals and how you plan to reach them is vital. Your team will trust you more when they know what to expect from you.

A leader demonstrates trust through their actions rather than their words. Reliability, hearing others' voices and vulnerabilities, and regular attendance cultivate trust. Creating a garden and cultivating trust are similar tasks that require time, attention, and the knowledge that what you plant today will grow tomorrow. Building a trusting atmosphere gives teams a sense of empowerment and belonging, stimulating creativity and teamwork.

Expertise and experience are the next steps in earning credibility. Demonstrating your knowledge and skills while remaining open to learning and growth showcases your commitment to excellence. Integrity, or doing the right thing even when no one is watching, solidifies your reputation as a leader worth following. By weaving transparency into your leadership approach, you invite open dialogue, reinforcing your credibility and deepening the trust others place in you.

The interplay between trust and credibility is a delicate dance requiring self-awareness and awareness of others' needs and perceptions. You can maintain this balance by actively listening, showing empathy, and being consistent in your words and actions. Embrace feedback, admit mistakes, and always strive for improvement. This will enhance your leadership profile and inspire those around you to reach their full potential.

It's about knowing your stuff and not being afraid to share your knowledge while acknowledging the expertise of relationship-building strategies:

- **Follow Through:** If you say you will do something, do it. Consistency in your actions reinforces reliability.
- **Open Communication:** Keep your team informed about successes and setbacks. Transparency fosters trust.
- **Encourage Peer-to-Peer Recognition:** Implement systems or forums where team members can acknowledge each other's efforts, achievements, and support. This can be as simple as a shout-out during meetings or a dedicated channel on team communication platforms.

Facilitating mutual support is about creating an environment where team members feel secure, valued, and connected. By implementing these strategies, you can build a resilient and collaborative team poised to achieve remarkable results together.

Key 2: Leading with Gravitas

This is my favorite topic. To influence effectively, you need to communicate in a way that resonates, persuades, and motivates. This is where gravitas comes into play—that intangible quality of being taken seriously and commanding respect and attention when speaking. Persuasive communication isn't about dictating; it's about engaging in a dialogue, understanding the perspectives of others, and compellingly presenting your ideas.

Gravitas, often shrouded in mystery, is the unnoticed theme of leadership. It has an aura that commands respect and attention, even when it doesn't say a word. Building up your gravitas is a journey of empowerment for women leaders, combining grace and strength. Let's investigate how you can improve your leadership by utilizing this potent quality.

At its core, gravitas is about confidence and poise under pressure. It's the weight of your presence in a room, the authority of your voice in discussions, and the calm in the storm. Cultivating gravitas involves a deep understanding of your values, a commitment to your vision, and the courage to stand firm in your beliefs. It's about mastering the art of spoken and unspoken communication, ensuring your message is heard and felt.

To develop gravitas, women must also navigate prejudices and stereotypes and turn them into chances to rethink leadership. The first step is to be self-aware and understand how your unique talents fit into your leadership style. Accept who you are, and let that serve as your direction. Communicate assertively, openly, and firmly about the concepts you believe in. Gravitas also shows how you encourage others, promoting an inclusive and respectful culture. You may improve your leadership presence and set an example for others by living up to these ideals.

Leading with gravitas as a woman today involves embodying a presence that commands respect and attention, combining depth of knowledge and expertise with the ability to communicate effectively and inspire others. Gravitas is about projecting confidence and authority while remaining authentic and approachable.

Applying the Approach

- **Know Your Audience:** Tailor your message to your listeners' interests, needs, and values. The more relevant your message is, the more impactful it will be. By doing this, you guarantee that your message not only reaches its target but also resonates, thereby enhancing its effectiveness.
- **Use Stories and Examples:** People connect with stories. Sharing real-life examples can help illustrate your points and make them more relatable.

Key 3: The Secret to Powerful Leadership: Emotional Brilliance

Once a peripheral concept, emotional intelligence (EI) has now taken center stage in leadership. It's the ability to be aware of, control, and express one's emotions and to handle interpersonal relationships judiciously and empathetically. Daniel Goleman, a pioneer in EI research, posits that emotional intelligence is as important as intellectual ability, if not more so, in determining leadership success. Why? Because the essence of leadership is not just about making decisions or setting strategies; it's about connecting with real people.

Due to their ability to negotiate the complexities of human emotions, leaders with high emotional intelligence are skilled at inspiring their colleagues, settling disputes, and fostering a good and productive work environment. They know people with goals, anxieties, and motives and create every email, spreadsheet, and project plan. Emotionally savvy leaders usually cultivate a climate of trust and respect by appealing to these human qualities, which encourages strong performance and loyalty. We will dive deeper into this in a later chapter.

WHAT EMOTIONAL INTELLIGENCE HAS TO DO WITH INFLUENCE

Emotional intelligence is the secret sauce of effective influence. It allows you to read the room, understand what drives the people you're trying to influence, and adjust your approach accordingly. High EI leaders are adept at managing their own emotions and recognizing and responding to the feelings of others. This ability to connect on an emotional level can significantly amplify your influence.

Here are a couple of anthologies that delve into the importance of using emotional intelligence at work:

Anthology 1: "Leading With Heart—The Power of Emotional Intelligence in Leadership"

This anthology illustrates how emotional intelligence can transform leadership styles, improve team dynamics, and enhance organizational culture. The anthology is divided into several sections, each focusing on different components of EI, including self-awareness, self-regulation, motivation, empathy, and social skills, and their impact on leadership effectiveness.

- **The Essence of Emotional Intelligence:** Introduces the concept of EI and its relevance to leadership. It explores how self-awareness forms the foundation of effective leadership.

- **Building Emotionally Intelligent Teams:** Focuses on the role of EI in team dynamics, including conflict resolution, communication, and collaboration.
- **Cultivating an Emotionally Intelligent Organization:** Discusses strategies for embedding EI into organizational culture, from hiring practices to professional development programs.

Anthology 2: "Empathy at Work— Enhancing Relationships and Results"

This anthology compiles insights from psychologists, business leaders, and HR professionals on the role of empathy in the workplace. It argues that empathy is a soft skill and a critical tool for building strong relationships, understanding customer needs, and driving innovation. The anthology is structured to provide readers with practical advice on developing empathy and leveraging it for personal and organizational success.

- **Understanding Empathy:** Defines empathy and distinguishes it from sympathy, focusing on its importance in the professional context.
- **Empathy in Action:** Shares stories of how empathy has led to breakthroughs in customer service, product development, and conflict resolution.
- **Developing Empathetic Leaders:** Offers guidance on nurturing empathy in leaders, including exercises and habits that help enhance emotional understanding.
- **The Outcomes of Empathy:** This chapter delves into the broader advantages of a compassionate work environment, including higher levels of employee involvement, dedication, and creativity.

Work quality will increase when a job is performed in an environment of mutual trust and cooperation between co-workers and employers. People become enthusiastic because they are happier together; this happiness shows itself as increased efficiency plus better cooperation from subordinates. Additionally, influence in the workplace fosters a sense of autonomy and recognition, directly contributing to overall happiness and job satisfaction among employees.

Self-regulation, another aspect of EI, involves managing your emotions to align with your values and the situation. It's about choosing your response rather than being at the mercy of your immediate reactions. This ability to pause and reflect before acting is crucial, particularly during stressful times, to ensure that your decisions and actions are thoughtful and purposeful. It means choosing a response instead of being subject to immediate reactions. This ability to delay action and consider it first is crucial, especially in times of stress when your decisions are made deliberately rather than hastily.

By combining these emotional intelligence components, you may build a resilient tapestry that enhances the lives of the people you lead and supports your leadership path. It's an ongoing development process in which every setback turns into a lesson, every setback lays the groundwork for future achievement, and every obstacle presents a chance to show off resilience's strength.

To boost your EI, consider these practices:

- **Practice Self-awareness:** Reflect on your feelings and actions to cultivate self-awareness. Learning more about who you are makes controlling your reactions much simpler.
- **Awaken Your Empathy:** Imagine yourself in another

person's shoes. Understanding their perspective might guide your communication and persuasion.

- **Engaged listening:** Pay attention not just to the words being said but to the emotions behind them. It is good to focus on the person's feelings and words. Acknowledging people's perspectives requires active listening.

Understanding your principles and objectives will keep you motivated and focused, even in the face of setbacks. This internal drive guarantees you stick to your course and overcome obstacles with grit and optimism.

Leadership influence has little to do with authority; it's about inspiring action, creating consensus, and guiding your team toward shared goals. It's built on a foundation of trust and credibility, enhanced through persuasive communication, and deeply rooted in emotional intelligence. By focusing on these areas, you become a more effective leader and a respected and trusted one.

3.2 ADVOCACY: A TOP LEADERSHIP TOOL

Advocacy is woven throughout the leadership skill set like a colorful thread that can characterize the entire piece. It's advocating for your group and bringing attention to their accomplishments, needs, and efforts inside and outside the larger company. Advocating for your team means that you are their biggest supporter; you are a champion who sees their potential and works to ensure that others do, too.

Throughout my nearly thirty-year career, numerous leaders have advocated on my behalf. To say that this contributed to my professional advancement would be an understatement. It is gratifying when senior and experienced individuals consider you for a new position, either by putting your name in the hat or sharing information with you.

Advocating Through Collaboration Over Competition: Changing the Narrative

Advocacy is critical to advancing women in leadership. It's about lending your voice and influence to create opportunities for yourself and other women striving to lead. Advocacy can take many forms, each significant in shaping a more inclusive future.

A paradigm shift in professional and personal advancement is under-way, a call to arms for women across generations to embrace collaboration over competition. This narrative is not just a whisper in the corridors of power but a loud, resonant voice echoing through women's lives.

The traditional view, framing competition as the only path to success, has served to isolate rather than uplift. It has painted success as a zero-sum game where one's gain must come at another's expense. However, this perspective needs to be updated and is fundamentally flawed. The truth, borne out by countless stories of women who've reached the zenith of their careers, is that collaboration is the secret sauce to achieving lasting, meaningful success.

Consider for a moment the power of a network where women support, mentor, and uplift each other. In such a network, knowledge is not hoarded but shared generously, opportunities are not gatekept but distributed widely, and success is not a solitary peak but a plateau where there's room for many to stand. This is not just an ideal but a practical strategy that has propelled women to heights previously unreachable.

Take, for example, the story of a tech entrepreneur who found her footing in a male-dominated industry not by guarding her trade secrets but by sharing them with fellow female entrepreneurs. Or the narrative of a young author who broke onto the scene, not by viewing other authors as rivals but as comrades-in-arms, together navigating the publishing labyrinth. These stories are not anomalies; they are beacons guiding us toward a future where collaboration over competition is the norm.

Applying the Approach

- **Sponsorship:** Offer guidance and support to emerging women leaders. Share your insights, provide constructive feedback, and, when possible, sponsor their advancement by recommending them for opportunities.
- **Visibility and Representation:** Be visible in your advocacy efforts. Speak at events, contribute to industry publications, and participate in forums focused on women's leadership. Your visibility underscores your commitment and encourages other women to take leadership spots.

The narrative of women's success is being rewritten, and collaboration is its central theme. By advocating for and practicing collaboration over competition, we change our trajectories and contribute to a broader cultural transformation. This is more than a strategy for success; it's a manifesto for a more inclusive, equitable, and flourishing society. Together, let's change the narrative.

The Importance of Advocating for Your Team

When leaders advocate for their teams, they perform several critical roles simultaneously: motivator, protector, and connector. By publicly recognizing team members' talents and achievements, leaders boost morale and directly contribute to their teams' professional growth. This recognition often translates into higher organizational visibility, opening doors to new opportunities and resources.

Practical Steps

- **Team Recognition:** Make it a habit to spotlight your team's accomplishments in company-wide meetings or newsletters. A simple shout-out can do wonders for someone's visibility.
- **Resource Acquisition:** Use your influence to secure the necessary resources for your team. This might mean arguing for budget increases, better tools, or more personnel.
- **Career Development:** Advocate for your team's professional development. This could mean recommending them for high-profile projects or supporting their case for promotions.

Promoting Diversity and Inclusion: The Function of Advocacy

Fostering diversity and inclusion is a moral imperative and a strategic advantage in today's corporate environment. In this endeavor, advocacy plays a crucial role, especially in amplifying the voices of those who might otherwise go unheard or marginalized. Leaders have the unique opportunity to advocate for policies and practices that promote a more inclusive workplace where everyone, regardless of their background, has the chance to thrive. If you manage global teams, this will be valuable for you.

Practical Steps

- **Celebrate Diversity:** Recognize and celebrate team members' cultural holidays, traditions, and milestones. This will honor their heritage and enrich your team's cultural tapestry.
- **Amplifying Voices:** Ensure that everyone on your team has a seat at the table. This means actively inviting input

from all team members and amplifying those voices in more extensive discussions, particularly those of underrepresented individuals.

- **Language Consideration:** Use clear, inclusive language and avoid jargon that might not be universally understood. Provide translation or interpretation services if necessary.
- **Time Zone Inclusivity:** Schedule meetings and deadlines with consideration for the various time zones of your global team members to ensure everyone can participate without undue hardship.
- **Safe Spaces for Dialogue:** Create forums or channels where team members can express concerns, share experiences, and discuss diversity and inclusion issues openly and safely.

Advocacy is about believing in your team's potential and using your position to ensure they have everything they need to succeed. It's about being their champion in every arena, fighting for their visibility, resources, and growth opportunities. This advocacy not only empowers individuals but can also catalyze significant changes in the culture and values of the entire organization, leading to a more inclusive, dynamic, and thriving workplace.

Supporting diversity and inclusion in global teams also needs a deliberate, thoughtful approach that considers the unique challenges and opportunities of having a diverse workforce. These strategies will make the international team setting more open, creative, and cohesive.

Encouraging Open Dialogue and Feedback

Creating a space where every voice feels heard and valued is not just about fostering communication but producing an environment where dialogue and feedback are the lifeblood of the team's ecosystem. Engaging in meaningful conversations that welcome and encourage diverse opinions is the essence of open dialogue.

Conversely, feedback acts as a mirror, reflecting the strengths and areas for growth within the team. Establishing mechanisms that facilitate this exchange in a way that feels constructive and empowering is crucial. Consider implementing regular feedback sessions that are structured yet open-ended, allowing team members to share their thoughts freely. Additionally, anonymous feedback tools can provide a platform for more candid insights, ensuring everyone feels comfortable voicing their opinions.

A culture that champions dialogue and feedback is one where growth can be continuous. This environment views mistakes not as setbacks but as chances for growth and development. This openness not only accelerates personal development but also drives the collective advancement of the team.

Advocacy and the Importance of Empathy

At the heart of advocacy lies empathy, the ability to understand and share another person's feelings. Empathy is the bridge that connects a leader's intention to advocate with the actual impact of those efforts. When leaders approach advocacy with empathy, they tailor their support to their team members' needs and aspirations. This empathetic approach ensures that advocacy efforts are well-intentioned and genuinely compelling.

Empathy in advocacy also means recognizing and addressing the unique challenges and barriers different team members face. It involves listening deeply to understand these challenges and acting thoughtfully to mitigate them. Whether advocating for flexible working arrangements for a team member with caregiving responsibilities or supporting the career advancement of underrepresented employees, empathy ensures that advocacy efforts are inclusive and impactful.

Moreover, leading with empathy fosters a culture of trust and belonging. When team members feel understood and supported, they are more engaged, committed, and motivated to contribute their best. Thus, empathy not only enriches advocacy efforts but also strengthens the very fabric of the team.

The Impact of Advocacy on Employee Engagement and Retention

Advocacy is a powerful tool for enhancing employee engagement and retention. When team members feel supported and championed by their leaders, their connection to the team and organization deepens. This sense of belonging and recognition fuels engagement, driving employees to invest more fully in their work and the team's collective goals.

Additionally, advocacy is essential for retention. In a market where talent is abundant, an employee's decision to remain with a company can significantly influence their sense of worth and encouragement. Advocacy communicates to employees the value of their contributions and the existence of advancement opportunities within the organization. This encourages people to stay, develop, and accept new challenges from the company.

The ripple effects of advocacy on engagement and retention are far-reaching. Engaged employees are more productive, innovative, and committed to excellence. Their enthusiasm and dedication can elevate the entire team, creating a cycle of positive reinforcement that drives success. Additionally, high retention rates contribute to a stable, experienced team capable of tackling complex challenges and achieving long-term goals.

In weaving a culture where open dialogue, empathy, and advocacy are cornerstones, leaders lay the groundwork for an effective, deeply connected, and resilient team. This foundation of support and understanding fosters an environment where every member feels valued and empowered to reach their full potential. The impact of such a culture extends beyond the immediate team, influencing the broader organization and setting a standard for genuinely inclusive and empowering leadership.

Through advocacy, you create a corporate culture that welcomes and does champion women in leadership. It's about dismantling barriers and building bridges, ensuring that leadership reflects the diversity and richness of perspectives that women bring.

As we move forward, let's carry these insights with us, recognizing that our role as leaders is not just to direct but to uplift, advocate, and connect. By embedding these principles into our leadership approach, we can create teams that are not only successful but also vibrant, inclusive, and deeply engaged.

Influence and advocacy work together to form a sophisticated tango that moves gracefully and purposefully across the streets of grassroots movements and the corridors of power. They are the creators of reality; they have a bold and strategic vision that they use to shape the present and the future. They embrace the challenge of the status quo and cultivate the seeds of change, nourished by an unwavering faith in the prospect of a better tomorrow. The fabric of human contact becomes more prosperous, more varied, and immeasurably more beautiful due to advocacy and influence, giving voices that were before marginalized a voice in the light.

CHAPTER 4
HARNESSING THE POWER OF NETWORKING

"Contrary to popular belief, the best way to reach the top of the ladder is to take others with you."

MARIA EITEL (FOUNDER AND CHAIR OF THE NIKE FOUNDATION, 2008)

Consider yourself the responsibility of the conductor, except in the context of orchestrating global networks, connections, and relationships rather than musical notes. The symphony of influence is not just about gathering individuals—it's about creating meaningful harmonies that empower, inspire, and drive you toward leadership excellence.

4.1 CIRCLES OF INFLUENCE: BUILDING YOUR LEADERSHIP NETWORK

Networking, often seen as a buzzword in business circles, is one of the most potent tools in a leader's toolkit. Building a diverse and dynamic network is more than just exchanging LinkedIn profiles at events, as it can unlock new opportunities and ideas, thereby fostering personal growth.

Crafting your leadership network is about more than amassing contacts; it is about building meaningful connections. It starts with a genuine interest in others, listening to their stories, and finding mutual grounds for support and collaboration. Attend industry events, join professional forums, and engage in discussions that matter to you and your circle. Remember, networking is a two-way street; focus on how you can also add value to others' lives. By encouraging these relationships, you create a resilient web of support that thrives on mutual respect and shared growth.

Your leadership network is a dynamic resource that evolves with your career. Leverage it by seeking mentorship, soliciting feedback, and collaborating on projects that challenge you. Don't shy away from introducing connections who can benefit from each other, as it strengthens your network's fabric. Embrace the diversity of your circles, allowing the varied perspectives to broaden your horizons. Remember, a well-developed network accelerates your growth and amplifies your impact.

Actionable Tip

Attend events outside your immediate industry. Why not check out a healthcare innovation conference if you're in tech? The cross-pollination of ideas can be surprisingly enlightening.

Effective Networkers' Practice of Active Listening

Listening more than talking is the key to successful networking. Listening is more important than talking when you're networking. Active listening allows you to understand the needs, goals, and challenges of others, creating a foundation for strong, mutually beneficial relationships. It's not about waiting for your turn to speak but genuinely engaging with the other person's ideas and thoughts.

Active listening is a pivotal skill in networking, especially for leaders striving to build meaningful connections and foster collaborative environments. As a female leader, I've found that embracing active listening can significantly enhance the quality of professional relationships and open doors to opportunities that might otherwise remain hidden. It goes beyond merely hearing words; it involves fully concentrating on the speaker, understanding their message, providing feedback, and retaining the information shared. In networking contexts, this skill demonstrates respect and genuine interest in the other person, which can be incredibly powerful in establishing trust and rapport.

Here are some ways in which active listening plays a crucial function in networking:

- **Building Deeper Connections:** Actively listening to the other person's thoughts and opinions facilitates the formation of deeper, more lasting connections. People are more likely to engage and feel heard and understood.
- **Identifying Opportunities:** Engaged listening lets you catch subtle cues and underlying messages indicating opportunities for collaboration, partnerships, or new ventures. Reading between the lines of explicit statements often yields these insights.

- **Enhancing Learning:** Every interaction in networking can be a learning opportunity. You gain knowledge through attentive listening and reflecting on new information, perspectives, and ideas, which can enrich your knowledge and understanding of various subjects and industries.
- **Improving Problem-Solving:** By listening actively, you might identify challenges and pain points that others face, presenting an opportunity to offer solutions or assistance. This strengthens relationships and positions you as a go-to resource within your network.
- **Facilitating Mutual Support:** Networking is about what you can gain and offer. Active listening enables you to understand the needs and goals of others, allowing for a more reciprocal and mutually beneficial networking dynamic. Facilitating mutual support in leadership is crucial for fostering a collaborative and resilient environment where people feel valued, supported, and motivated.

At your next networking event, challenge yourself to ask open-ended questions and listen to the answers. You might be surprised by what you learn and how it deepens your connection.

4.2 BUILDING YOUR LEADERSHIP NETWORK

Developing a robust network is akin to planting a garden. It requires intention, care, and a bit of creativity to flourish. In this garden, mentors and allies are your perennial plants, providing stability and growth year after year. Multi-sector connections are especially the seasonal blooms that add diversity and color, while professional associations are the trellises that support and elevate the entire garden. Let's explore how to plant and nurture these essential elements in your leadership network garden.

Leveraging Social Media for Networking

Social media platforms like LinkedIn and Instagram can be powerful networking tools. They allow you to connect with global leaders and peers worldwide, share insights, and engage with your field's latest trends and ideas.

Share an article or study you found thought-provoking on LinkedIn and add your perspective. Tag the author and others in your network to start a conversation. This shows you're engaged with current trends and helps establish your voice in the community.

Networking isn't just a skill—it's an art. By building diverse connections, practicing active listening, and leveraging social media, you'll create a harmonious orchestra of influence that supports your growth and enriches your entire ecosystem.

Identifying Potential Mentors and Allies

Finding the right mentors and allies is about recognizing those individuals whose experience, wisdom, or position can help guide and elevate your career. These are the people who have navigated the path you're on and have insights to share. However, searching for mentors and allies goes beyond looking for titles or accolades. It's about finding individuals who resonate with your values and understand your vision for the future.

Practical Steps

- Start by mapping out your career goals and the areas where you seek growth or guidance.
- Look for individuals in your industry or company who embody the qualities you admire or have achieved similar goals.

- Don't restrict your quest to superiors. Peers or people close to you can provide highly insightful viewpoints, particularly while navigating the latest trends and technologies.
- The Power of the Pack—Women Supporting Women: Building a network of mentors, peers, and supporters can provide the encouragement, advice, and perspective needed to navigate challenges. The strength of sisterhood will bring you to new heights of collaborative success and collective empowerment.

Establishing a relationship with a potential mentor or ally begins with a genuine connection. Reach out with specific questions or requests for advice based on their expertise, and always be well prepared ahead of time. Show appreciation for their time and clarify that you're seeking a mutually beneficial relationship, not just a one-way flow of guidance.

Cross-Industry Networking Is Powerful: Professional Groups Can Help You Network

While it's natural to gravitate towards networking within your industry, going outside this comfort zone can be incredibly rewarding. Cross-industry networking brings fresh perspectives, stimulates innovation, and can uncover opportunities you might not have found otherwise. It challenges you to think differently and apply lessons from one field to another.

By embracing cross-industry networking, you may inspire yourself to solve problems in a novel way and bring fresh perspectives to your job. It's about adding other perspectives and opinions to your network so you may be inspired and move forward.

Professional associations are a nexus for individuals passionate about their careers and personal development. These organizations offer a structured way to connect with peers, mentors, and industry leaders. They're not just about attending conferences or seminars; they're communities where you can engage deeply with your profession and the people who shape it.

Practical Steps

- Identify associations that align with your career goals and interests. Many offer specialized groups or committees you can join, providing more intimate networking settings.
- Get involved beyond just being a member. Volunteer for an initiative, offer to speak at an event or write an article for their website. Active participation raises your profile and opens up more opportunities for meaningful connections.
- Use the resources and platforms provided by these associations. Many have online forums, job boards, and mentorship programs to help members connect and support each other.
- Join online forums or social media groups focused on topics of interest but outside your industry. Engage in discussions, share your insights, and connect with members who pique your interest.
- Consider volunteering for organizations or causes that align with your values but are not directly related to your profession. This can be a rich ground for meeting diverse individuals who can broaden your perspective. These are wonderful places to meet individuals who can offer new insights and ideas.

Professional associations give you a platform to showcase your expertise, learn from others, and build connections to support your career over the long term. They offer a blend of formal and informal networking opportunities, making finding and fostering relationships with individuals who share your interests and aspirations easier.

My adventure has been gratifying as an enthusiastic member and leader of PMI, Project Management International. Over the years, my involvement with PMI has grown from being a dedicated member to achieving respected accreditation and even stepping up to serve on the local chapter's board of directors as a spirited volunteer. This journey has been a delightful blend of networking, discovery, and friendship. The countless individuals I've met, each bringing their own stories, dreams, and ideas, have greatly enriched my professional life, adding joy and satisfaction. These interactions have not only expanded my professional circle but have also turned into enduring friendships. The chance to work with, learn from, and be inspired by so many passionate professionals has been a highlight of my career, turning my time with PMI into a cherished part of my story, filled with laughter, education, and lasting connections.

In sum, building your leadership network is a deliberate and dynamic process. It involves seeking mentors and allies who can guide and support you, embracing the diversity of cross-industry connections, and leveraging the structure and opportunities provided by professional associations.

4.3 TAKING CARE OF YOUR NETWORK CONNECTIONS

Building a network is like planting a garden—the care after planting brings the blooms. Nurturing your network relationships is where the actual growth happens, turning connections into allies, collaborators, and even lifelong friends. This nurturing requires a mindful approach, focusing on reciprocity, sustained effort, and regular touchpoints to keep the relationships vibrant and beneficial.

During my career, one of my superpowers has been networking and connecting with other like-minded people. Their connections often evolve into long-lasting alliances, coaching relationships, and occasionally close friendships that help people work through professional and personal growth challenges. It brings me great joy to see these relationships grow over time. It captures what it means to be a leader: making a lasting impression on people's lives and leaving a legacy of harmony, development, and support for one another. This facet of leadership involves uplifting others and fostering a culture that prioritizes cooperation over rivalry in addition to one's achievement.

Paying it Forward in Networking

Reciprocity acts as the soil that nourishes your network garden, creating an environment where support and generosity flow freely. This mutual exchange is about more than keeping score; it's about fostering a culture of giving and receiving. When you approach your network with a mindset of how you can help others, not just what you can gain, you plant seeds of goodwill that often grow into opportunities and support when you least expect it.

Practical Steps

- Offer your skills or time to someone in your network without expecting anything in return. This could be as simple as providing feedback on a project, sharing an article relevant to their work, or offering an introduction.
- When you receive help or advice, look for ways to express your gratitude and consider how to pay it forward. This might mean helping someone else in your network or

finding a way to support the person who assisted you in a new way.

Keys to Maintaining Long-Term Professional Relationships

The strength of your network isn't measured by the number of connections but by the depth of those relationships. Maintaining these bonds over the long term requires consistent effort and recognizing that professional relationships, like personal ones, evolve.

It is expected that both sides will benefit from the connection. Give as much assistance as you receive. When two of your connections could benefit from working together, introduce them to each other. As a result, a network of helpful professionals can emerge. Adding a personal touch to business interactions can be as simple as remembering someone's birthday or asking about their family.

To keep your professional ties strong over the long haul, you must work hard, commit, and honestly desire to see your network succeed. If you pay attention to these factors, you can build relationships that help you professionally and personally, which will help you advance in your career.

Practical Steps

- Make a habit of contacting your connections regularly, even when you don't need anything. A simple message checking in or sharing something of interest can warm the relationship. One of my favorite things is to ask different people to lunch once a month. It keeps me connected to them, and I can hear their latest adventures.
- Celebrate their successes, offer support during challenges, and stay curious about their projects and growth. This

ongoing interest shows that you value the relationship for
more than just professional gain.

- Be understanding and flexible as careers and lives evolve.
  While how you connect and support each other might
  change, the underlying relationship can remain strong if
  nurtured.

Mastering the Art of Consistent Communication: Unlocking the Power of Networking

Regular communication is the water that keeps your network thriving. It's about staying present and engaged, ensuring your connections are active and meaningful. In today's digital world, there are countless ways to keep in touch, but the key is choosing genuine methods that suit the nature of each relationship.

Talking isn't communication; it's about building trust and relationships and ensuring everyone feels like they belong and are informed.

Mastering the art of consistent communication comes down to ensuring everyone feels valued and heard, keeping things real, and ensuring they are essential. There needs to be more than just sharing information; you also need to ensure everyone is on the same page and working toward the same goals. Keep it simple, informal, and free of misunderstandings.

Practical Steps

- Whether it's weekly one-on-ones or team meetings, keep
  them regular and adapt when needed.
- Be there fully when you're in a conversation or meeting. It's
  like showing up to a coffee date with a friend and enjoying
  the coffee together.

- Use social media to celebrate the achievements of your connections and stay informed about their career developments. A quick comment or share can go a long way in showing your support.
- Schedule regular catch-ups or check-ins with crucial contacts, whether a brief phone call or a face-to-face meeting, when possible. These interactions provide an opportunity for more personal updates and deeper conversations.
- Keep notes on essential details from your interactions (such as their interests, career goals, and personal milestones) and use these to add a personal touch to your communication. This shows you're listening and caring about them beyond the professional sphere.

Nurturing your network is an ongoing process that requires thoughtfulness, consistency, and a genuine interest in the growth and well-being of those within it. By focusing on reciprocity, maintaining long-term relationships, and ensuring regular communication, you create a network that's not just wide but deep—filled with meaningful, supportive, and enduring connections.

As we wrap up this networking and relationship-building exploration, remember that these connections are more than just a means to a professional end. They're the community supporting, challenging, and growing with you throughout your career. The effort you invest in nurturing these relationships pays dividends in ways that are often unexpected but always invaluable. With your network garden flourishing, you're well-equipped to face the challenges ahead, knowing you have a wealth of resources, wisdom, and support at your fingertips.

We are moving forward on this adventure, exploring new leadership and personal development horizons. Every relationship and encounter you have is a step towards new opportunities, leading by example, inspiring others to join in the quest for excellence and growth.

CHAPTER 5

WALKING THE TIGHTROPE OF LEADERSHIP

"To me, leadership is about encouraging people, stimulating them, and enabling them to achieve what they can—and do that with a purpose."

CHRISTINE LAGARDE (PRESIDENT OF THE EUROPEAN CENTRAL BANK, 2019)

Consider a tightrope walker in a circus act. The safety net appears a long distance below them. Every step is calculated and intentional. A collapse is possible if they slant too much to one side; an overabundance of confidence and overcorrection could have the same deadly effect. Balance is vital in this act, and dynamic, ongoing adjustment must be maintained.

Now that you're thinking about leadership and life consider this: Our ability to adapt and establish steadiness in the face of turmoil constantly keeps us solid, not the lack of movement. This is our daily tightrope walk between work and life.

5.1 THE DELUSION OF PERFECT BALANCE

Talk of work-life balance often conjures images of a perfectly calibrated scale where professional responsibilities and personal life sit harmoniously. However, balance is not a map's final destination or fixed point. It's more akin to how the weather changes every day as a result of numerous factors both under and outside of our control. Striving for a perfect balance is like chasing the end of a rainbow; it's an exercise in futility and frustration.

Alternatively, think about work-life harmony, which recognizes the interdependence of our personal and professional lives. On certain days, work requires all our focus; other days, personal obligations come first. Instead of giving each the same amount of time, the objective is to establish a long-term, satisfying rhythm.

5.2 THE MYTH OF PERFECT BALANCE: EMBRACING WORK-LIFE INTEGRATION

In today's always-connected world, the lines between work and life blur more efficiently than ever. Emails arrive at all hours; remote work means our offices are often just steps from where we sleep. Work-life integration recognizes this reality and seeks to weave our professional and personal lives together in a way that feels authentic to us. It's about creating a life where work enhances our personal experiences and vice versa, rather than the two being in constant competition.

There are practical steps we can take to manage this integration. One approach is setting boundaries around work—specific times when we're available and not—and communicating these boundaries clearly to colleagues and loved ones. Another is making space for personal passions and interests, even scheduling them into our calendars with the same non-negotiable status as a work meeting. This intentional approach to integration acknowledges that while work is a significant part of our lives, it's not the only part.

If we can't find a good balance between our work and home lives, it can negatively affect our health, relationships, and ability to lead. Stress, burnout, and chronic fatigue can cloud judgment, dampen creativity, and reduce our capacity to lead with empathy and insight. Moreover, leaders set the tone for organizational culture; if we're visibly overworked and stressed, our teams know this is acceptable and expected. If you are consistently staying late and working weekends, and your team sees this continuous behavior, they will, in turn, often feel they need to follow your lead.

Conversely, leaders who model healthy work-life integration inspire their teams to find equilibrium. This can lead to a more energized, focused, and productive workforce. Encouraging your team members to take time for rest and personal pursuits isn't a sign of leniency; it's an investment in your team's long-term health and success. Obtaining a work-life balance can be tricky, yet it is well worth the effort for everyone.

The tightrope walk of leadership and life demands balance and the agility to navigate the inherent fluctuations. By shifting our aim from the elusive ideal of perfect balance to the more practical, dynamic approach of work-life integration, we equip ourselves to lead not just with effectiveness but with sustainability and joy. This is the leadership tightrope walk—constantly adjusting, always moving forward.

Consequently, pursuing perfection in this area often leads to frustration. Instead, work-life integration offers a more fluid approach, recognizing that priorities shift and the boundaries between work and personal life sometimes blur.

Practical Steps

- **Acknowledge the Fluidity of Priorities:** Some weeks are more work-heavy, while others may allow more personal time. This perspective helps manage expectations and reduces the guilt of not achieving a perfect balance.
- **Leverage Technology Wisely:** Technology can tether us to work and offer flexibility. Use it to your advantage by working remotely when needed or using apps to streamline tasks, freeing up time for personal pursuits.
- **Set clear limits:** Establish and communicate your limits with your team and family. This could involve setting specific work-free hours or disconnecting during vacations. You can encourage others to do the same by honoring these boundaries yourself.

5.3 BRIDGING THE GAP: PERSONAL AND PROFESSIONAL DEVELOPMENT

Striking a harmonious balance remains a top aspiration for many in the dynamic interplay of leading a fulfilling life and forging a successful career. This section delves into the nuances of aligning personal passions with professional ambitions, rethinking the concept of work-life balance, and spotlighting the fundamental role of self-care for leaders aiming high.

Aligning Personal Passions With Professional Goals

When personal interests and professional objectives align, work transcends being a means to an end. It becomes a source of joy and fulfillment. Achieving this synergy starts with a deep dive into understanding what drives you and what causes excitement and purpose in you.

Practical Steps

- **Identify Your Passions:** List activities that make you lose track of time or those you would do even if you were not being paid for them. These are clues to your passions.
- **Set Professional Objectives That Reflect Your Passions:** Next, envision how these interests can intersect with your career. For some, it might mean transitioning to a role involving their passions. For others, it could entail incorporating elements of their interests into their current position through side projects or initiatives.
- **Communicate Your Aspirations:** Share your vision with mentors, supervisors, or HR. Their insights could open doors to opportunities aligned with your interests, projects, training, or lateral organizational moves.

5.4 PRIORITIZING SELF-CARE AND MENTAL WELL-BEING: STRATEGIES FOR THE AMBITIOUS LEADER

For ambitious leaders, self-care is not a luxury but a necessity. It's the fuel that powers the drive to achieve lofty goals.

In the high-stakes realm of leadership, the pressure to constantly perform at peak levels can often lead to neglect of one's own mental health and well-being. However, for the ambitious leader, prioritizing self-care is not a luxury but a critical strategy for sustaining long-term effectiveness and resilience. A leader who embodies this principle integrates structured self-care routines into her daily life, recognizing that mental fortitude is the bedrock of her ability to inspire, innovate, and lead with empathy. This includes setting aside time for mindfulness practices to maintain clarity of thought, engaging in regular physical activity to bolster physical and mental health, and ensuring adequate rest to rejuvenate the mind and body. Furthermore, fostering strong support networks, both professional and personal, provides a safety net that can offer guidance, feedback, and the emotional sustenance necessary to navigate the challenges of leadership. The ambitious leader enhances her well-being and sets a powerful example for her team by championing self-care, thereby promoting a culture that values mental health as a critical component of success.

Practical Steps

- **Schedule Time for YOU:** Block off time for activities to replenish your energy as you schedule a meeting. This could be exercise, meditation, hobbies, or time with loved ones.
- **Mindfulness Practices:** Incorporating mindfulness into your daily routine can enhance mental clarity and reduce stress. Techniques such as deep breathing, meditation, or even mindful walking can be powerful tools for well-being.
- **Seek Support When Needed:** Leadership can be isolating, making it all the more important to have a support system. This could be a professional mentor, a coach, or a peer support group. Don't hesitate to seek professional help if you're struggling with stress or mental health issues.

Navigating the complexities of personal and professional development is an ongoing process. It requires introspection, a willingness to adapt, and the courage to pursue what truly resonates with your core values. By aligning your passions with your career, embracing the fluidity of work-life integration, and prioritizing your well-being, you pave the way for a fulfilling leadership journey that does not compromise your happiness for professional success.

In wrapping up this exploration into personal and professional development, we lay the groundwork for the next steps in our leadership journey. It's a reminder that our careers are not just about our titles but about creating lives rich in purpose, fulfillment, and well-being. As we move forward, let's carry these insights with us, using them to mold the leaders we become and the lives we lead.

5.5 STRATEGIES FOR CULTIVATING SELF-AWARENESS

Self-awareness is the cornerstone of emotional intelligence and is pivotal to personal growth and professional leadership. It is the conscious knowledge of one's character, feelings, motives, and hopes. Leaders who cultivate self-awareness step into authentic leadership characterized by genuine interactions, ethical decision-making, and a profound ability to inspire and motivate others.

Regular self-reflection practices like journaling, meditation, or thinking about one's behaviors and experiences can significantly enhance self-awareness. By intentionally pausing in a hectic world, you can be afforded the opportunity to examine your daily experiences critically, derive lessons from them, and deliberate on future actions and reactions.

Self-Awareness

To be a good leader, you must first be self-aware, which means you must be aware of your personality, emotions, motivations, and desires. Building self-awareness is especially helpful for women in leadership positions.

Reflective Practices

Reflective practices are essential to professional development and personal growth, especially for leaders. These practices involve thinking critically about one's actions, decisions, and experiences to gain deeper insights into one's behavior, motivations, and the outcomes of one's actions. For women in leadership, reflective practices can be precious, enabling them to navigate the complexities of their roles with greater awareness and adaptability. Below, we explore various contemplative practices and their effective implementation.

Journaling

Journaling is a powerful tool for reflection. It involves writing down thoughts, experiences, and feelings about daily events, interactions, and decisions. For leaders, journaling can help process complex situations, identify patterns in behavior or decision-making, and track personal growth over time. It is a private space where leaders can freely explore their successes and challenges, enhancing their self-awareness and emotional intelligence.

Reflective Discussion Groups

Engaging in reflective discussion groups can provide a supportive environment for sharing experiences and challenges. These discussions encourage leaders to articulate their thoughts and feelings, gain insights from the experiences of others, and receive diverse perspectives on their situations. This collective reflection can be enriching, offering multiple lenses through which to view one's leadership journey.

Implementing Reflective Practices

To effectively implement reflective practices, leaders may want to:

- **Set aside dedicated time:** Regularly schedule time for reflection, whether daily, weekly, or after significant events.
- **Create a reflective routine:** Find a reflective method that resonates with you personally, such as journaling, meditation, or group discussions, and make it a consistent part of your routine.
- **Be open and honest:** Reflection is most effective when you are truthful about your feelings, thoughts, and actions.
- **Use reflection for action:** Translate insights gained from reflective practices into actionable personal and professional development steps.

Incorporating reflective practices into one's leadership approach enhances self-awareness and fosters a culture of improvement. For women in leadership, these practices are invaluable tools for navigating the complexities of their positions with insight, resilience, and strategic foresight.

CHAPTER 6

GROWTH MINDSET FOR LEADERSHIP

"I learned always to take on things I'd never done before. Growth and comfort do not coexist."

GINNY ROMETTY (CEO, IBM, 2011)

Navigating the unpredictable tides of the corporate world calls for a mindset that welcomes and thrives on the unexpected. This section delves into the core aspects of such a mindset: embracing challenges and change, harnessing the power of positive thinking, and the indispensable role of perseverance and resilience.

Carol Dweck, a psychologist, developed the concept of a growth mindset. Through commitment, hard work, and proper training, she believes one can develop one's intellect and ability. A fixed mindset, on the other hand, holds that skills and intelligence are unchangeable and undevelopable traits.

6.1 MODEL AND REWARD A MIND READY FOR GROWTH

Leaders should model the growth mindset behaviors they wish to see, demonstrating an openness to learning and a willingness to tackle challenges head-on.

Reward and recognize behaviors that exemplify a growth mindset, such as taking on new challenges, learning from mistakes, and persevering in adversity.

You can frame and support women in leadership in a way that fosters a growth mindset, creating more resilient, dynamic, and successful leaders by incorporating the principles outlined in this book into your organizational culture.

6.2 MASTERING THE STAGE: PUBLIC SPEAKING AS A LEADERSHIP TOOL FOR YOUR GROWTH JOURNEY

Public speaking is one of the most influential tools at a leader's disposal, capable of inspiring teams, advocating transformative changes, and establishing an individual as a thought leader within their industry. Once you master this skill, no one can take it away from you. This chapter delves into the art and science of harnessing public speaking, not just as a means of communication but as a strategic leadership instrument that can elevate your influence and effectiveness. Learning this skill can enhance self-confidence and adaptability, key components of a growth mindset.

The Power of Preparation

The foundation of compelling public speaking is thorough preparation. Knowing your material inside out enables you to speak confidently, ensuring that you can handle questions or challenges gracefully. Preparation extends beyond familiarity with your content;

it involves understanding your speech's context, your audience's needs and expectations, and the key message you wish to convey. This meticulous preparation lays the groundwork for an informative but also engaging and persuasive presentation.

Engaging Your Audience

To connect with your audience confidently, integrate stories illustrating your key points. Stories can make your speech more relatable and impactful, transcending data or theoretical concepts. These narratives can anchor your message to real-world experiences, making abstract ideas tangible and memorable. Additionally, judicious use of visuals can significantly complement your spoken words. Visual aids should enhance your message, not distract from it, so it's crucial to use them sparingly and ensure they are directly relevant to your points.

Overcoming Fear and Anxiety

For many, the thought of public speaking evokes fear and anxiety. However, overcoming these feelings can unlock unparalleled influence and career advancement opportunities. I assure you that this one skill will place you above the rest. Regular practice in low-stakes environments is invaluable for building confidence. This practice allows you to refine your delivery, adapt to unexpected situations, and receive constructive feedback in a supportive setting. Visualization techniques, where you imagine a successful presentation, can also help cultivate a positive mindset and reduce pre-speech anxiety. Furthermore, participation in groups or workshops focused on public speaking, such as Toastmasters International, offers a structured environment to develop your skills and gain confidence through practice and feedback.

Connecting With Your Audience

Effective public speaking transcends the mere delivery of information; it involves creating a genuine connection with your audience and moving them to action. To achieve this, tailor your speech to align with the audience's interests, concerns, and level of understanding. This alignment ensures your message is heard and resonates deeply with your listeners. The strategic use of pauses can enhance the impact of your message, providing the audience with moments to absorb and reflect on the information shared. Finally, concluding your speech with a clear call to action is paramount. This directive should guide your audience toward the desired thoughts, feelings, or actions you wish them to take following your presentation, ensuring your message has a lasting and actionable impact.

When mastered, public speaking is a critical leadership skill that can significantly enhance your ability to inspire, influence, and lead. Through meticulous preparation, engaging storytelling, overcoming personal barriers, and a deep connection with your audience, public speaking becomes not just a method of communication but a powerful tool for leadership and change.

6.3 NAVIGATING THROUGH OBSTACLES AND TRANSFORMATION

Visualize standing at the foot of a mountain, its peak obscured by clouds. For some, this sight is daunting—a signal to turn back. For leaders with a growth mindset, however, it's an invitation to climb and discover what lies beyond their current vantage point. This mindset transforms obstacles into stepping stones, seeing them not as barriers but as opportunities to expand one's capabilities and impact.

Applying the Approach

- **Adopting a Learner's Perspective:** Every challenge presents a chance to gain new knowledge or skills. Adopting this perspective turns potential setbacks into valuable lessons.
- **Flexibility in Strategy:** Being rigid when facing challenges is a recipe for frustration. Flexibility allows leaders to alter paths, finding new and sometimes better routes to their goals.
- **Welcoming Change:** Change is inevitable in a constantly evolving world. Leaders who embrace change position themselves and their teams to capitalize on new opportunities and innovations.

6.4 STRATEGIES FOR SUSTAINING CONFIDENCE IN HIGH-PRESSURE SITUATIONS

Confidence in High-pressure Situations

Confidence is not just a state of mind; it's a powerful determinant of success in high-pressure situations. Whether you're about to deliver a crucial presentation, compete in a significant business proposal, or make an important decision under tight time constraints, your confidence level can dramatically influence the outcome. High-pressure situations magnify our doubts and insecurities, leading to decreased performance. Understanding how to sustain confidence in these moments is crucial for anyone looking to excel in their respective fields.

Preparation and Practice

One of my favorite TED talks is by Julian Treasure, "How to speak so that people want to listen." He provides expert advice on how to speak with empathy and more. His voice exercises are priceless.

The foundation of confidence is preparation. Familiarity with the task at hand reduces anxiety and increases self-assurance. Regular, deliberate practice, especially under conditions that simulate a high-pressure environment, can significantly enhance one's confidence. For instance, public speakers often rehearse in front of friends or cameras to mimic the feeling of being on stage. Athletes practice under various scenarios to prepare for the unpredictability of the game. This strategy improves skill levels and builds a mental frame-work that associates the high-pressure situation with familiarity rather than fear.

Positive Self-talk and Mental Rehearsal

The dialogue you have with yourself during high-pressure events can either uplift or undermine your confidence. Transforming negative thoughts into positive affirmations is a powerful tool for sustaining confidence. Phrases like "I am prepared" or "I can handle this" before you start that presentation or business pitch can significantly alter your mental state. Mental rehearsal, or visualizing successful outcomes, further solidifies your belief in your ability to perform under pressure. Athletes and performers widely use this technique to mentally prepare for their events, thereby enhancing their confidence and performance.

Breathing Techniques and Relaxation Exercises

Physical symptoms of stress, such as rapid heartbeat and shallow breathing, can intensify feelings of anxiety and pressure. Mastering the art of breathing control can have an immediate calming effect. Techniques such as deep, box, and diaphragmatic breathing can help maintain a sense of peace. Reducing stress and encouraging an optimal mental state will lead to better performance.

Stretching, going for a brisk stroll outside, and other activities can also be considered forms of relaxation.

Setting Realistic Goals and Embracing Failures

An environment that recognizes achievements and views failures as opportunities fosters the growth of confidence. Setting small, achievable goals can provide a sense of progress and accomplishment, building confidence over time. Equally important is the ability to view failures not as reflections of personal inadequacy but as invaluable feedback for improvement. This outlook encourages perseverance and a constructive mindset when confronted with obstacles.

Social Support and Professional Guidance

A supportive network of friends, family, mentors, or coaches can significantly impact your confidence. These individuals provide encouragement, advice, and constructive feedback, helping you navigate through pressures with a positive outlook. In cases where anxiety or stress becomes overwhelming, seeking professional guidance from psychologists or counselors trained in performance psychology can be beneficial.

Sustaining confidence in high-pressure situations is a multifaceted endeavor that requires mental, emotional, and physical strategies. By incorporating thorough preparation, positive self-talk, effective stress-reduction techniques, realistic goal setting, and seeking support, individuals can significantly enhance their ability to perform confidently when it matters most. Over time, you can develop and strengthen your confidence, turning pressure into an opportunity for greatness.

6.5 UNLEASHING THE POWER WITHIN: HOW OPTIMISM CAN TRANSFORM LEADERSHIP

When it comes to leadership, where challenges and choices come at you like a hurricane, there is an untapped source of power that can change the course of lives: the unstoppable force of positive thinking. It's not enough to see the glass as half full; you have to know that the glass can be filled again, that every setback is a way to make a come-back, and that every problem lies in a chance just waiting to be found.

The lens through which leaders view their environment can dramatically affect their effectiveness and team morale. Positive thinking is not about ignoring reality or the challenges it presents. It's about maintaining a hopeful outlook that energizes and motivates, turning potential hurdles into manageable tasks.

Optimism, that bright thread running through a woman's work, isn't just a way to find her way; it's the light itself. Each strand of hope is so crucial that it would protect her on her way up the career ladder. The light that would lead her fearless self-closer to her goals. The one that tells you to turn left or right when the road seems blocked, and you think there's no other way to go.

During my career, I have heavily relied on thinking positively, reading inspirational books, and surrounding myself with supportive individuals, all of which have been crucial to my professional success. When we choose to be optimistic, we stay alive and grow, leaving a mark on the world that will last longer than the hands of time.

Practical Steps

- **Having a Can-Do Attitude:** This contagious mindset inspires teams to approach tasks enthusiastically and confidently.
- **Visualizing Success:** Positive thinking often involves visualizing the desired outcome. This practice can clarify the steps needed to achieve success and maintain focus when faced with obstacles.
- **Reframing Challenges:** Positive thinking reframes challenges as puzzles to solve, infusing creativity and determination into the problem-solving process.

6.6 CONNECT TO ELEVATE: TRANSFORMING LEADERSHIP THROUGH INTERPERSONAL MASTERY

Amidst the ever-changing fabric of business executives, where strategic acumen and visionary foresight are often acclaimed as the hallmarks of success, the subtle yet profound influence of interpersonal skills emerges as a pivotal, though frequently underappreciated, thread. The essence of leadership transcends the mere orchestration of tasks; it is fundamentally about forging connections, understanding hearts, and aligning minds. Women in corporate leadership positions have been instrumental in spotlighting this truth, demonstrating with remarkable clarity how interpersonal skills are not just supplementary but central to crafting a cohesive leadership strategy and nurturing a thriving team. Their approach, rich in empathy and attuned to the nuanced spectrum of human emotions, starkly contrasts the traditional, more transactional leadership paradigms, which prioritize results over relationships. With their innate propensity for empathy, active listening, and emotional intelligence, these women leaders illuminate a path where a team's strength stems from its unity and the depth of its connections.

The significance of interpersonal skills in leadership is multifaceted, encompassing the ability to communicate effectively, resolve conflicts with grace, and inspire trust and loyalty. Women leaders use these skills to foster an environment that fosters dialogue, encourages the free exchange of ideas, and values diverse perspectives. This contrasts sharply with environments where communication is top-down and one-dimensional, leading to a culture of silence rather than innovation. A woman who cherishes interpersonal connections leads a vibrant team where each member feels seen, heard, and valued. This is a team where motivation springs not from fear of failure but from the genuine desire to contribute to a shared vision.

Moreover, the art of conflict resolution, where interpersonal skills shine brightly, becomes a cornerstone of effective leadership. Instead of viewing conflicts as battles to win, women in leadership positions view them as opportunities for growth and understanding. Through empathetic engagement and active listening, they navigate disagreements, ensuring that the outcome strengthens rather than weakens team cohesion. This ability to transform potential discord into a catalyst for stronger bonds is a testament to the power of interpersonal skills in maintaining the fabric of a united team.

Trust, the invisible glue that holds teams together, is another dimension where the impact of interpersonal skills is profoundly visible. Women leaders, with their authentic and transparent approach, foster an atmosphere of trust and security. Their leadership style, consistent openness, and genuine care for team members' well-being generate a culture of loyalty and commitment. This stands in marked contrast to leadership styles that rely on hierarchy and control, which may achieve compliance but rarely engender genuine commitment. In the nuanced dance of leadership, where every gesture and word has the power to influence, women leaders demonstrate that trust is earned through the consistent application of interpersonal skills, weaving a more substantial and resilient team fabric.

The contribution of women leaders to redefining leadership through the prism of interpersonal skills is a vibrant narrative of transformation. They have demonstrated that cultivating relationships with care, respect, and understanding is the foundation for outstanding leadership and team success. In doing so, they challenge the conventional wisdom that views emotional intelligence and relational abilities as secondary to technical expertise. Instead, they assert that these skills enable leaders to navigate the complexities of the corporate world, achieve strategic objectives, and, most importantly, unleash the full potential of their teams.

In a world increasingly recognizing the limitations of rigid, command-and-control leadership models, women leaders' emphasis on interpersonal skills offers a refreshing and compelling alternative. This leadership approach doesn't just aim for targets but cherishes the journey, recognizes the value of each team member, and builds a collective strength that can weather the storms of the corporate sea.

To summarize this chapter, the leadership growth mindset is characterized by an openness to learning, a positive outlook, and an unyielding commitment to one's goals. This mindset transforms potential leaders into impactful ones capable of navigating the complexities of the corporate world with grace and determination.

CHAPTER 7

THE POWER OF STRENGTHS IN LEADERSHIP

"Women have always been the strong ones in the world."

COCO CHANEL (FRENCH FASHION DESIGNER)

Visualize that you're at a buffet with various dishes from around the globe. You've got a plate in your hand, and here's the catch—you can only pick the dishes that truly delight your taste buds. This scenario is much like leading with your strengths. It's about focusing on what you naturally excel at rather than trying to fill your plate with everything available. This approach not only makes leadership more fulfilling but also more rewarding.

In a world that often emphasizes improving weaknesses, spotlighting our strengths can feel counterintuitive. Yet, it's through leveraging these innate talents that leaders can inspire, motivate, and drive their teams to new heights. After all, our strengths set us apart, define our unique leadership style, and enable us to make our most significant contributions.

7.1 STRENGTHS-BASED LEADERSHIP APPROACH

Identifying Your Strengths

The journey to identifying your strengths starts with a mix of self-reflection and feedback from others. Think about the tasks that energize you, where time flies, and when you're most creative and productive. These are clues to your inherent strengths. Tools like the CliftonStrengths assessment can offer insights. Furthermore, don't underestimate the value of simply asking colleagues and friends when they've seen you at your best. CliftonStrengths, a philosophy and tool developed by Gallup, identifies 34 distinct strengths across four domains: Strategic Thinking, Influencing, Relationship Building, and Executing.

Understand Your Strengths

- **Complete the CliftonStrengths Assessment:** Take the CliftonStrengths assessment to identify your top strengths. Understanding these will give you a clear picture of where your natural talents lie.
- **Reflect on How You Use Your Strengths:** Consider how your strengths play out in your day-to-day activities. Reflecting on instances where you've successfully used your strengths can help you understand how to apply them more deliberately.

Action Step

At the end of each day for a week, jot down the moments you felt most engaged and fulfilled at work. Look for patterns to identify your strengths further.

Leveraging Strengths in Leadership

Once you know your strengths, the next step is to weave them into your leadership style. Match your strengths to the demands of leadership positions and tasks. For instance, if "Achiever" is one of your top strengths on CliftonStrengths, you bring a lot of energy and a strong work ethic to your leadership job. Because you naturally like to set and beat goals, you inspire your team to do even better, which leads to their success as a whole.

Identify challenges where your strengths can be particularly effective. Instead of trying to improve in areas where you are weak, use your strengths to approach these challenges from a different angle.

Strengths and Development for Your Team

Developing your strengths within the team further means pushing beyond your comfort zone to apply them in new and challenging contexts. Encourage your group to attend workshops, seek mentorship, or take on projects that stretch you and your abilities in areas where everyone can excel. The goal is to deepen your expertise and versatility in using your strengths, not to rest on your laurels.

Practical Group Steps

- **Identify the Strengths of Your Team Members:** Encourage your team to take the CliftonStrengths assessment and share their results. Understanding each other's strengths can foster appreciation, reduce conflict, and improve collaboration.

- **Assign Roles Based on Strengths:** Allocate tasks and responsibilities according to each team member's strengths. This ensures that everyone works in their area of greatest potential, leading to increased engagement and productivity.
- **Encourage Strengths Development:** Promote the ongoing development of each team member's strengths. Offer opportunities for training, mentoring, and projects that align with their strengths.
- **Celebrate Strengths in Action:** Recognize and celebrate when team members use their strengths effectively. This reinforces the value of a strengths-based approach and encourages its continued use.

The shift toward a strengths-based approach in leadership is more than just a strategy; it's a mindset change. It's about recognizing that our most significant potential lies in doing more of what we naturally do best. This doesn't mean ignoring weaknesses but building a team where diverse strengths complement each other, covering gaps. When leaders and their teams operate from a place of strength, the result is a more engaged, productive, and resilient organization.

In today's fast-paced and complex business environment, playing to your strengths and encouraging your team to do the same isn't just sensible; it's essential. When we shift our focus towards growing our innate leadership strengths, we unlock a realm of untapped potential. It's akin to nurturing a garden; with suitable attention and resources, what already has the promise to bloom can transform into something truly magnificent. This growth, however, only happens in collaboration. It thrives on a diet of continuous learning, receptive feedback, and the guided insights of coaching. Each element plays an integral part in enhancing our strengths and ensuring they can navigate the complexities of leadership in today's dynamic corporate landscape.

Action Plan

Pick one key strength and set a goal to use it more effectively in your leadership position over the next month. Track your progress and the impact on your team.

7.2 AGILITY: REVOLUTIONIZING LEADERSHIP NOW

In today's fast-evolving business terrain, pivoting and adapting swiftly is not just valuable; it's paramount. This necessity births the concept of agile leadership, a style that champions rapid response to change over following a set plan. It's about leaders who anticipate shifts in the landscape and thrive amidst them, ensuring their teams remain productive and engaged.

Agile development principles, initially designed for software projects that prioritize flexibility, collaboration, and customer satisfaction, form the foundation of agile leadership. When applied to leadership, it underscores a dynamic approach where decision-making is fluid, strategies are adaptable, and learning from each iteration is crucial.

Understanding Agile Leadership

At its core, agile leadership is characterized by a willingness to remain open to new information and to adjust accordingly. It's a mindset that views change not as a hurdle but as an opportunity for growth and innovation. This perspective requires a departure from traditional leadership models that rely heavily on hierarchy and rigid planning.

Key attributes of an agile leader include

- A focus on fostering a culture of trust and empowerment where team members are encouraged to take initiative and make decisions.
- Commitment to constantly improve and learn at an individual and team level.
- Flexibility in thought and action allows quick adaptation to changing circumstances without losing sight of overarching goals.

Benefits of Agile Leadership

Adopting agile leadership can transform the workplace in numerous ways, enhancing performance and satisfaction. Many people say that the idea of speed in leadership is like how water flows. It's about going with purpose, adapting to the environment, and figuring out the best way to move forward, no matter what comes up. As time passes, the only thing that stays the same is change. Adapting quickly to new situations is not a luxury; it's a requirement. Knowing how to use disruption to spark new ideas, solve problems quickly, and put together a team that loves being flexible and wants to do more than live in a constantly changing world is essential.

Applying the Approach

- **Enhanced Responsiveness and Transparency:** Agile leaders and their teams can react swiftly to shifts in the market, customer preferences, or technological advancements, maintaining a competitive edge.
- **Increased Innovation:** Agile leadership encourages experimentation and learning from failures, paving the way for breakthrough ideas and solutions.

- **Higher Employee Engagement:** Promotes autonomy and values input from all team members.
- **Improved Customer Satisfaction:** Teams led by agile leaders are better positioned to meet and exceed customer expectations by focusing on delivering value and adapting to feedback.

Agile Decision-Making

A hallmark of agile leadership is making informed, timely decisions that propel the team forward. This approach to decision-making is iterative, with each choice serving as a learning point for the next.

The nuanced approach of incorporating diverse perspectives into the decision-making process marks the hallmark of an agile leader. This methodology underscores the importance of engaging with a wide array of viewpoints to cultivate a comprehensive understanding of the challenges and opportunities that lie ahead. An inclusive approach guarantees the enrichment of decisions through the diverse insights and experiences to which each team member contributes.

Agile leadership also places a premium on flexibility, acknowledging the fluid nature of the business environment. Despite their decisive nature, decisions are open to reevaluation and adjustment in response to new information or changing circumstances. This adaptive mindset allows leaders to remain resilient and responsive, navigating their teams through the unpredictable waters of corporate life with agility and anticipation.

After reaching a decision, the focus quickly shifts to swift and efficient execution. Agile leaders understand that the value of a decision lies in its implementation. Prompt action fosters an environment that maintains momentum and seizes opportunities. However, this quick execution does not preclude the possibility of adjustments. On the contrary, we anticipate making refinements as the situation develops, thereby boosting the agility of the leadership approach.

An intrinsic element of agile leadership is the emphasis on learning. Every outcome, whether a triumphant success or a humbling setback, is perceived as a valuable source of insight. Agile leaders embrace these experiences as opportunities to deepen their understanding and refine their strategies. This commitment to continuous learning and development fosters a culture of improvement and innovation within the team. It equips leaders with the wisdom and adaptability needed to thrive.

Through agile decision-making, leaders ensure their teams are not just reacting to changes but actively leveraging them to create value and drive progress. This dynamic process underscores the essence of agile leadership: the ability to navigate the intricacies of the contemporary business landscape with anticipation, adaptability, and fortitude.

As the business world transforms, the mantra of leadership agility becomes increasingly pertinent. "Embracing agility" is not just about surviving in a world of change; it's about thriving, leading with vision and flexibility, and building resilient, innovative, and prepared organizations for the future. The journey towards agile leadership is ongoing and evolving, but it is undoubtedly the path forward for those seeking to lead with impact now.

7.3 FUTURE-PROOFING PRINCIPLES

The principles below follow steps to future-proof your journey as you navigate the leadership position. They will help to assure that, despite the difficulties that lie ahead, your distinctive narrative will be one of development, resiliency, and unrelenting dedication to changing the world. Your journey is full of possibility and promise, just like that of the main character in a great book. Accept it with bravery, interest, and a wide-open heart.

Continuous Learning

The world of business is always in flux, mirroring the rapid pace of change in the global business environment. Staying relevant, therefore, means committing to a path of never-ending learning. This pursuit is not just about accumulating knowledge. We strive to enhance our comprehension, hone our abilities, and broaden our viewpoints to maintain a competitive edge in a constantly evolving field. This desire to learn is like that of a great author who continuously improves their skills to ensure their work stays exciting and relevant.

Applying the Approach

- **Expand Beyond Your Field:** Look for learning opportunities that stretch beyond the immediate boundaries of your industry or expertise. Engaging with diverse topics sparks creativity.
- **Leverage Technology:** Make the most of digital platforms offering courses, webinars, and podcasts. These resources can provide flexible learning options that fit around your commitments.
- **Create a Learning Circle or Book Club:** Surround yourself with peers who share your enthusiasm for growth. This circle can become a source of encouragement, challenge, and exchange, pushing you to learn more deeply and broadly apply your insights.

Seeking Feedback

Feedback is the mirror that helps us grow. Feedback provides insight into the perception of our leadership, its influence, and the areas where we excel. Embracing feedback, especially when it challenges our self-perception, requires courage. Yet, through this openness to hear and adapt, growth occurs appropriately.

Practical measures towards creating a growth- and innovation-friendly atmosphere are crucial to increasing women's representation in business leadership positions. A culture of transparency is fundamental to these activities. In such an environment, people can speak their minds without worrying about the consequences. The abundance of insights gained is beneficial and revolutionary when team members are comfortable expressing their thoughts and views. Team members can understand one another better and work together due to this free flow of information.

Leaders should aim for targeted questions rather than broad ones to further hone this feedback culture. Even though it's courteous, general feedback rarely gets to the heart of the matter and provides little practical advice. On the other hand, asking for input on specific decisions or situations can provide practical and constructive solutions. This degree of detail allows for a more deliberate and targeted discussion, giving leaders the information they need to make wise decisions.

Nevertheless, gathering feedback is just the beginning of the adventure. What follows is where the meat of the issue lies. The leader is responsible for sorting the useful comments from the irrelevant ones. With this ability to discriminate, they can find the truth among all the false information. Taking action is the next stage. Armed with this knowledge, leaders must make meaningful and purposeful adjustments. They show their dedication to development and create an atmosphere that celebrates and encourages growth by using feedback to improve things. Especially for women navigating the complicated waters of corporate leadership, this feedback, reflection, and action cycle is a potent weapon in any leader's toolbox. These are the real-world actions leaders may take to motivate their people to innovate and thrive.

Leadership Coaching

Joining forces with a like-minded individual who can push us to our limits and help us succeed is often the best method to take our careers to the next level. Leadership coaching offers this partnership, providing a tailored approach that maximizes our personal and professional potential. A coach helps identify and develop our strengths and uncovers blind spots and limiting beliefs that may hold us back.

Practical Steps

- **Choose the Right Coach:** Find a coach whose expertise aligns with your growth objectives. The right fit is crucial, as this relationship is built on trust and mutual respect.
- **Engage Fully in the Process:** Coaching requires active participation, follow-up, and planning. Approach each session with openness and a willingness to explore even the uncomfortable corners of your leadership style.
- **Apply Insights:** The actual value of coaching is realized by applying insights gained. Between sessions, actively work on the areas identified, experimenting with new strategies and behaviors.

In essence, building confidence as a growing female leader is a dynamic process that thrives on continuous learning, clear feedback, and guidance from coaching. This trifecta enhances your inherent abilities but equips you to navigate the complexities and demands of leadership in today's world. Committing to this growth path elevates your leadership and inspires those around you to embark on their journey.

7.4 VENTURING INTO THE THRILL OF TRANSFORMATION

Change is the only constant in today's corporate environment. Technological advancements and shifts in consumer behavior constantly present leaders with new challenges and opportunities. Welcoming change rather than resisting it requires a mindset shift. It's about viewing change not as a threat but as an opportunity for growth and innovation.

Cultivate curiosity about emerging trends and developments in your industry. This proactive stance can be transformational in that it assists in anticipating changes rather than reacting to them.

Communicate openly with your team about the inevitability of change. Encourage them to share their thoughts and feelings about upcoming transitions.

Demonstrate resilience. Show your team that while change can be challenging, it's also an opportunity to learn and become stronger.

Adapting to change is not just about survival; it's about seizing opportunities to lead more effectively and creatively. It's about setting a course that acknowledges the winds of change and uses them to propel your team forward.

Agile Problem-Solving

When faced with challenges, agile leaders employ a problem-solving approach that is both creative and pragmatic. Rapid iteration characterizes this approach, leading to the rapid development, testing, and refinement of solutions. It's about making informed decisions based on the best available data and adjusting those decisions as more information becomes available.

Use brainstorming sessions to generate a wide range of solutions. Encourage all team members to contribute, fostering a culture of valuing every idea.

Prioritize solutions based on impact and feasibility. This helps focus efforts on the most promising options. Implement solutions in stages, assessing results at each step. This iterative process allows for continuous improvement and adjustment.

Agile problem-solving turns obstacles into opportunities for innovation. It encourages a culture of experimentation, where learning and adaptation are integral to finding the best path forward.

Fostering an Agile Team

We utilize agile problem-solving to transform challenges into opportunities for innovation. It fosters an environment open to experimentation, where learning and adaptability are essential in determining the most effective way to proceed.

Practical Steps

- Promote a culture of trust and psychological safety where team members feel free to express ideas, take risks, and voice concerns without fear of judgment or retaliation. Such a culture encourages open communication, risk-taking without fear of failure or retribution, and sharing ideas and challenges.

- Encourage people from different job areas to work together. By breaking down barriers between groups and encouraging them to work together, you can promote new ideas and make solving problems easier.
- Invest in training and development that boosts agility. This includes technical and soft skills such as communication, collaboration, and adaptability.
- React constructively to mistakes. When errors occur, focus on learning and improvement rather than assigning blame. This approach encourages innovation and experimentation by removing the fear of failure.
- Offer support and resources. Provide resources and support for personal and professional development. Investing in the growth of team members fosters a sense of value and trust.

An agile team is a resilient team. It's a collective that can confidently and creatively navigate the complexities of the modern business landscape, turning challenges into victories and uncertainty into opportunity.

Leading with agility in a rapidly changing world is about more than just being flexible or quick to adapt. Creating an environment that welcomes change, approaches challenges with innovative thinking, and empowers teams to move confidently and creatively is the key. It's about recognizing that, in the fluid dynamics of today's corporate world, agility is not just a strategy but a fundamental approach to leadership.

As we close this exploration of agility in leadership, it's clear that the principles of adaptability, creative problem-solving, and fostering a flexible team are more than just responses to the challenges of our time. They are proactive strategies for shaping a future where leaders and their teams survive and thrive. These principles guide us toward a vision of leadership that is dynamic, inclusive, and forward-thinking.

And now, we turn our gaze to the horizon, where the next chapter awaits, ready to reveal new perspectives and possibilities.

CHAPTER 8
SHAKING THE FOUNDATIONS— EMBRACING CHANGE IN LEADERSHIP

"Do what you feel in your heart to be right - for you'll be criticized anyway."

ELEANOR ROOSEVELT (FORMER FIRST LADY OF THE UNITED STATES)

Just picture yourself entering a place where every voice resounds with conviction and direction, whether loud or soft. This isn't just a space where communication happens; it's where transformation begins. In the corporate realm, creating such spaces isn't about rearranging the furniture; it's about rethinking the very essence of leadership. It's a shift from traditional command work to a dynamic, inclusive jam session where every participant brings their own unique rhythm. The urgency for this shift toward women leaders has never been more palpable, with diversity, inclusivity, and adaptability not just being nice-to-haves but absolute musts for navigating the complexities of today's business world.

8.1 THE DIRE NEED FOR DIVERSITY IN CORPORATE LEADERSHIP

Diversity in leadership isn't just about filling quotas or ticking off boxes on a checklist. It's an acknowledgment that diverse perspectives bring richness and depth to decision-making processes, encouraging new ideas and grit. Think of it this way: if a team comprises individuals who all think alike, they look at every problem and opportunity through the same lens. Trying to capture the entire landscape through a narrow tube leaves much unseen. Companies can gain a more complete picture of their environment, including its opportunities and threats, by increasing the diversity of thought within their executive ranks.

Companies with diverse leadership teams outperform their more homogeneous counterparts in sectors like tech and finance, where innovation is the lifeblood of success in terms of creativity and financial return.

The Impact of Inclusive Leadership

Inclusive leadership goes beyond having a heterogeneous team. It's about creating an environment where members feel valued, heard, and empowered to contribute their best. This type of leadership recognizes that diversity without inclusion is like having an orchestra without a conductor; the potential for harmony exists, but without guidance and encouragement, the music never takes flight.

The impact of inclusive leadership can be profound, spanning various aspects of organizational performance and culture. By encouraging team members from varied backgrounds to share their perspectives, organizations can tap into a wealth of creative solutions that might not emerge in a more uniform setting.

For example, if a multinational technology firm implemented diverse brainstorming sessions led by an inclusive leadership team that encouraged participation from all levels of the organization. This approach could lead to a groundbreaking new product that combines insights from different disciplines, including engineering, marketing, and user experience design. The product may significantly outperform its predecessors, underscoring the direct link between inclusive leadership and innovation.

Inclusive leaders leverage the diverse perspectives within their teams to make more informed and balanced decisions. By considering various viewpoints, leaders can anticipate potential challenges and better utilize possibilities, leading to better outcomes.

Example

In the financial services industry, a firm's executive team, known for its inclusive leadership style, strategically decided to expand into a new market. The decision was informed by comprehensive input from team members who had direct knowledge of the market's cultural, economic, and regulatory landscape. This approach allowed the firm to avoid competitors' pitfalls and successfully establish its presence in the new market.

Inclusive leadership is not just a moral imperative but a strategic advantage. Leaders can drive better business outcomes by fostering an environment where diversity is valued and leveraged, from innovation and employee engagement to decision-making and customer satisfaction. The examples provided underscore the tangible benefits that inclusive leadership can bring to an organization, highlighting its importance in today's global and diverse business landscape.

The Power of Adaptability

As a female executive, you have a rare chance to mold your company's climate toward diversity and inclusion. Let's start by having conversations that promote various voices being heard and amplified. Establishing a secure environment where employees feel comfortable expressing their thoughts and opinions might help accomplish this goal. Encouraging safe spaces for staff to speak up helps the entire company.

In the corporate world, resistance to change is a common response. It's the human tendency to cling to the familiar, even when it's clear that the status quo is no longer serving us well. However, embracing change isn't just about keeping pace with the market or technological advancements; it's about actively seeking ways to improve and develop into a more capable leader.

The call for diversity, inclusivity, and adaptability in leadership is not just a response to the changing landscapes of industries worldwide. It's a recognition of the untapped potential that lies in reimagining the foundations of leadership itself. In this chapter, we delve into the practical steps and strategies leaders can employ to navigate and drive change within their organizations, ensuring they're not just participants in the future of business but active shapers of it.

Remember that what you are creating is a mosaic of inclusivity, not merely a workplace and that each and every one of your employees is a vital piece. Change, diversity, and inclusivity in the corporate world are not just buzzwords but imperatives for those aiming to lead effectively in today's dynamic environment. By embracing these principles, leaders can create more resilient and innovative teams aligned with the multifaceted nature of the global market. The shift towards more diverse, inclusive, and adaptable leadership practices is not just a moral or ethical choice; it's a strategic one, laying the groundwork for companies that are both successful in the short term and sustainable and influential in the long run.

8.2 LEADING WITH VISION

In leadership, vision serves as the North Star, guiding the leader and the organization toward a defined future. Yet, having a vision is only part of the equation. The actual test of leadership lies in translating this vision into actionable strategies and adapting swiftly to the inevitable challenges. This segment explores the nuances of crafting a vision that inspires, aligning that vision with concrete actions, and navigating the twists and turns of the corporate landscape with agility and resolve.

A compelling vision goes beyond business goals; it encapsulates an organization's aspirations, values, and purpose. It's a vivid picture of the future that motivates the team and resonates with customers and stakeholders. Introspection, imagination, and knowledge about your organization's larger-effect goals are necessary for creating such a vision.

Applying the Approach

- **Begin with Your Why:** Clarify how you contribute to the organization's core purpose. Why does it exist beyond making a profit? This foundational 'why' becomes the cornerstone of your vision, imbuing it with meaning and direction.
- **Engage in Futuristic Thinking:** Allow yourself to dream big to allow for the best possible future for your organization, considering the impact of emerging trends and innovations. This process should be liberating, unbound by the constraints of current capabilities or challenges.

- **Make It Relatable:** Ensure your vision is articulated in a way that speaks directly to the hearts and minds of your team and stakeholders. It should be simple, straightforward, and capable of stirring enthusiasm and commitment.

By laying down an ambitious and purposeful vision, you set the stage for transformative leadership. This vision acts as a beacon, keeping the organization's journey aligned with its ultimate aspirations, even when the path becomes clouded by uncertainty or setbacks.

Aligning Vision With Action

Strategic, deliberate, and aligned actions build the bridge between vision and reality. Without this harmony, any aspiration would remain just that—a dream. Translating vision into action involves setting clear goals, rallying your team around these objectives, and establishing a culture that thrives on innovation and execution.

- **Break It Down:** Dissect your overarching vision into tangible goals and milestones. This breakdown transforms the vision from an abstract concept into a series of achievable steps, making it easier for your team to grasp and act upon.
- **Communicate and Collaborate:** Share your organization's vision and strategic goals widely. Encourage feedback and involve your team in refining the action plan. This collaborative approach ensures buy-in and enriches the plan with diverse perspectives.
- **Foster a Culture of Execution:** Cultivate an organizational culture that values execution as much as it does creativity. Acknowledge and reward progress towards goals, and ensure your team has the resources and autonomy to take initiative and make decisions.

In aligning vision with action, the role of a leader transcends from being a visionary to an orchestrator of change. It's about creating a dynamic where the vision guides, the strategy directs, and the team's collective efforts propel the organization forward.

There is no path to realizing a vision without its hurdles. Market shifts, technological advancements, internal dynamics, and countless other factors can challenge the most well-laid plans.

The capacity to adjust to unforeseen circumstances while maintaining focus quickly and efficiently on the goal is essential for overcoming these obstacles.

Practical Steps

- **Anticipate and Adapt:** Stay ahead of the curve by continuously scanning the external environment for potential disruptors. Use these insights to adapt your strategies proactively rather than reactively. This foresight allows for smoother navigation through challenges, minimizing disruptions to your strategic objectives.
- **Empower Your Team:** Equip your team with the skills and mindset to handle change. This involves training and fostering an environment that encourages experimentation and learning from failures. An empowered team is your best ally in responding to challenges with creativity and resilience.
- **Maintain Flexibility:** While the vision remains constant, the routes to achieving it can vary. Be willing to adjust your plans and strategies in response to new information or changing circumstances. Your ability to adapt will guarantee that your leadership continues to be effective, regardless of obstacles.

8.3 FROM STATUS QUO TO INNOVATION

Within the dynamic business realm, if you want your impact to last, you can't afford to put your feet up. The real challenge lies not in executing daily tasks but in breaking free from the comfort of the familiar to tread the uncharted territories of innovation. This section explores how leaders can act as catalysts for change, nurturing environments where creativity flourishes and guiding their organizations through transformative journeys.

As a female leader in the corporate world, disrupting conventional practices is not just a pathway to significant innovation; it's a necessary step toward fostering diversity, inclusivity, and resilience within organizations. Traditional leadership models often emphasize hierarchy, uniformity, and a singular approach to problem-solving, which can stifle creativity and hinder the development of a complex workforce. Challenging these norms opens the door to new perspectives, encourages collaborative problem-solving, and creates environments where diverse talents and ideas can thrive.

Disruptive leadership includes encouraging a culture of always learning, putting flexibility ahead of strict systems, and giving employees at all levels the freedom to share their ideas and take the lead. It involves rethinking communication channels, decision-making processes, and success metrics to be more inclusive and reflective of a dynamic global marketplace. It presents an opportunity for female leaders to redefine strength, assertiveness, and success in leadership positions. By leveraging our unique perspectives and experiences, we can lead change that transforms organizations and challenges societal perceptions of leadership.

Disrupting Conventional Practices

The first step in fostering a culture of innovation is to question the existing state of affairs. This doesn't mean dismissing every established process or tradition out of hand but rather adopting a mindset that is continually on the lookout for improvement.

Encourage your team to adopt this perspective by:

- **Creating a safe space for questioning:** Let your team know that every process is open to scrutiny, no matter how ingrained. This openness can reveal inefficiencies or outdated practices ripe for overhaul.
- **Rewarding curiosity:** When team members bring forward questions or suggest alternatives, recognize their initiative. This encourages a culture of inquiry and can lead to valuable insights and innovations.
- **Leading by example:** Show your willingness to challenge assumptions and decisions. By setting a powerful precedent, you signal to your team that you value adaptation and evolution.

Promoting Creativity

After challenging the status quo, the next step is actively supporting innovation. In this context, "welcoming new ideas" refers to cultivating an atmosphere where innovation is incorporated into the routine work process.

A few strategies include:

- **Dedicating resources:** Whether it's time during the workweek for creative projects or financial support for pursuing new ideas, tangible resources signal your commitment to innovation.
- **Mixing teams:** Cross-functional teams bring diverse perspectives together, sparking creativity. Encourage collaboration across departments to break down silos and stimulate new thinking.
- **Embracing failure:** Not every idea will pan out, and that's okay. Make it clear that failure is a part of the innovation process, a speed bump rather than a total setback. Celebrate the lessons learned from these attempts to encourage continuous experimentation.

Leading Organizational Change

Steering your organization through the waters of change requires more than a vision for the future. It demands a nuanced understanding of the dynamics at play within your team and the broader organizational culture.

Here's how you can guide your organization through this transformative process:

- **Communicate clearly and often:** Change can be unsettling. Keep your team informed about the reasons for change, the intended outcomes, and the steps along the way. Transparent communication helps mitigate anxiety and builds trust.
- **Engage champions of change:** Identify individuals within your organization who are particularly receptive to the

change or who stand to benefit significantly from it. These champions can help sway opinion and foster a more positive outlook on the transition.

- **Monitor and adjust:** Keep a close watch on how the organization is implementing the change. Be ready to tweak your approach based on feedback and the results you're seeing. This agility ensures the process aligns with your goals and team's needs.

As we wrap up this exploration into the role of leadership in guiding organizations from the familiar grounds of the status quo to the invigorating realms of innovation, a few key points stand out. First, the courage to question and the curiosity to explore are invaluable in uncovering opportunities for improvement and creativity. Next, we can transform these opportunities into tangible outcomes by fostering an environment that nurtures and celebrates innovation. Finally, leading organizational change with clarity, support, and flexibility ensures these innovations take root, driving the organization forward.

Moving from this chapter to the next, we understand that leadership is not a static place but a dynamic journey. It's about constantly seeking ways to improve, innovate, and lead by example, inspiring others to join in the quest for excellence and growth.

CHAPTER 9

THE BACKBONE OF LEADERSHIP— CULTIVATING RESILIENCE

"Life is just a journey."

DIANA (PRINCESS OF WALES)

Envision a grand oak tree, its limbs protruding into the atmosphere and its foundations firmly rooted in the ground. It adapts to the wind's direction while maintaining its ground during cyclones by bending but not breaking. The tree endures adversity and flourishes, deriving fortitude from such trials. Leadership resembles the relentless nature of an oak in numerous respects. Success in leadership remains contingent not on the absence of obstacles but on one's capacity to adapt, develop, and respond constructively amidst adversity.

9.1 LEADERSHIP AND THE VALUE OF RESILIENCE

Understanding Resilience

Resilience, in its essence, is about bouncing back from difficulties. That inner grit lets you face failures, setbacks, or adversity and say, "This won't define me. I will learn, adjust, and continue to move forward." Resilience is not inborn; it's developed through experiences and the conscious decision to tackle challenges head-on.

The importance of resilience in leadership cannot be overstated, especially in the dynamic and frequently unpredictable corporate world. Resilience, the ability to withstand, adapt to, and recover from adversity, is a cornerstone of effective leadership. It enables leaders to survive challenges, uncertainties, and failures and emerge stronger and more capable. Understanding resilience in leadership involves recognizing that setbacks and obstacles are not just barriers to success but opportunities for growth, learning, and innovation.

For a female leader, resilience is a personal journey and a necessary professional strategy. It's about cultivating an inner strength that allows vulnerability and learning from every experience. Resilience is characterized by flexibility, optimism, and the persistence to pursue goals despite difficulties. It's about building a supportive network that includes mentors, peers, and team members, fostering a culture of mutual support and shared success. This network becomes a source of strength, offering diverse perspectives and solutions in times of crisis.

Demonstrating how to face challenges with grace, learn from mistakes, and rebound from setbacks encourages a similar resilience mindset among team members. It promotes a mindset in the workplace that is open to change, always looking for ways to get better, and not afraid to take some measured risks. Understanding and embodying resilience enables leaders to inspire confidence, drive change, and cultivate an environment where innovation and creativity flourish.

Additionally, leadership resilience requires setting a positive example for those around you. We encourage team members to adopt a resilient mindset by demonstrating how to handle challenges with poise, grow from errors, and overcome obstacles. It fosters a culture within the company that values flexibility, continuous improvement, and the courage to take calculated risks. Leaders can instill confidence, facilitate change, and create an environment that encourages imagination and new ideas when they understand and exemplify resiliency.

Resilience enables you to navigate through any challenge and even learn to thrive in it. Success depends on knowing oneself, one's team, and the company's bigger picture. To create more inclusive, flexible, and prosperous companies, female executives in the business sector must embrace and demonstrate resilience.

Being Resilient as a Leader

When you're in charge, bouncing back positively is like having a compass that leads you and your team through the good and bad times. It influences how one handles stress, takes risks, and serves as an example to others. An enduring leader does more than ride out bad times; they use them to teach their team members to do the same. It's about showing that hard times aren't the end of the road but rather the beginning of something far better.

Think about every success story you've heard. Often, they're tales of overcoming adversity, not unchallenged triumphs. That's because resilience, focusing on growth and learning from failure, paves the way for genuine, lasting success. It builds a foundation of strength that no setback can shake, ensuring that you and your team become more assertive on the other side.

When the pressure mounts and obstacles seem insurmountable, your team looks to you for guidance. How you react affects the outcome and sets the tone for your team's approach to challenges. Resilience in leadership means maintaining a clear vision and a positive outlook, even when faced with setbacks. It's about showing your team that any obstacle can be overcome with perseverance and a positive attitude. This doesn't mean you ignore the reality of the situation or downplay the challenges. Instead, it's about approaching them with a mindset geared towards tangible solutions and growth.

Real-Life Example: The Resilient Leader

Think about a senior project manager named Kyra, who led her team through a high-stakes project that fell short of the client's expectations despite everyone's best efforts. The team was disheartened, doubting their skills and fearing the impact on their reputation. Here's where resilience turned the tide. Kyra gathered her team not to assign blame but to extract lessons. They dissected the project, pinpointing where things went wrong and brainstorming how to improve. Instead of letting this holdup define them, Kyra and her team used it as a catalyst for growth. They implemented new strategies and communication tools, significantly improving their workflow and efficiency. The next project was a success, not just in meeting the client's expectations but in surpassing them. This turnaround wasn't about luck but resilience—the decision to learn, adapt, and return stronger.

The Impact of Resilience on Success

Success is rarely a straight line. It's a winding path filled with hurdles, and resilience is the fuel that keeps you moving forward. It's what allows you to take risks, innovate, and pursue ambitious goals, knowing that failure is not the end but a part of the journey. An innovative culture can flourish when failures are seen as chances for learning and development, and a resilient leader can motivate their team to adopt this outlook. This culture makes things happen and helps build resilient teams within the corporate world.

Being resilient will help you face the difficulties you'll inevitably face as a leader and will give your team the edge they need to succeed in an ever-changing environment. Passing on resilience, flexibility, and determination distinguishes great leaders from the ordinary.

9.2 BUILDING YOUR LEADERSHIP RESILIENCE

Resilience-Building Strategies

Adopting specific strategies can significantly bolster your ability to bounce back when faced with the ebb and flow of leadership challenges. First and foremost, it's critical to establish a solid foundation of self-care. This isn't about indulgence but ensuring your physical and emotional well-being is complete, so you have the energy and clarity to tackle obstacles head-on. Regular exercise, adequate rest, and nutrition play pivotal roles, as does carving out time for activities that rejuvenate your spirit and mind.

Another critical strategy involves setting boundaries. In a world increasingly blurring the lines between work and personal life, knowing when to step back is crucial. These boundaries protect your time and energy, ensuring you're not spread too thin and can focus on what truly matters.

Building solid connections inside and outside your professional network offers priceless support when things get complicated. These relationships provide insight, counsel, and a sympathetic ear when difficulties emerge. They offer consolation and encouragement by reminding you that you're not traveling alone.

Refining a Resilient Mindset

The heart of strength lies not in the strategies we employ but in the mindset we enable. A resilient mindset sees obstacles as temporary and surmountable. It understands that failure is not a reflection of one's abilities but an opportunity for growth. To nurture this mindset, start by practicing gratitude. Focusing on what you're thankful for, even amid challenges, can shift your perspective from what's going wrong to what's going right.

As we discussed earlier, another component of a sturdy mindset is adaptability. The ability to pivot and adjust your plans in response to changing circumstances is invaluable. It involves staying open to new information and perspectives, even if they challenge your preconceptions. This flexibility ensures you remain effective, no matter what curveballs come your way.

9.3 TURNING TRIALS INTO TRIUMPHS

Trials are inevitable in life and in leadership. They can range from minor hiccups to monumental challenges that test our spirit, resolve, and character. How we face these obstacles can define our path forward, transforming potential defeat into a platform for outstanding development and achievement.

Navigating Setbacks

When confronted with setbacks, the initial reaction can often be frustration, disappointment, or even despair. However, the first step in navigating these challenges is to adopt a mindset that views setbacks not as insurmountable barriers but as opportunities for learning and growth. This perspective shift is crucial and sets the stage for a constructive approach to overcoming obstacles.

Practical Steps

- **Pause and Assess:** Give yourself ample space to absorb the impact of the setback. This pause allows for emotional processing and a more precise situational assessment.
- **Identify the Learning Opportunity:** Every setback carries a lesson. Understanding what went wrong, why it occurred, and how to prevent it in the future transforms the experience into a valuable learning opportunity.
- **Plan Your Next Moves:** With the insights gained from the setback, outline a plan of action. This plan should include immediate steps to stabilize the situation and long-term strategies to prevent similar setbacks.

Turning the Table

Deliberate actions and a steadfast commitment to your goals mark the journey from a setback to a comeback. This process involves addressing the immediate aftermath of the setback and laying the groundwork for more robust, more resilient leadership. The journey through the corporate landscape is rarely a straight line. Highs and lows, successes and failures mark it. It's. The difference between those who reach their leadership potential and those who falter often comes from perseverance and resilience.

Practical Steps

- **Implement the Lessons Learned:** Apply the insights from the setback to improve processes, strategies, or personal leadership approaches. This application demonstrates a commitment to growth and improvement.
- **Reaffirm Your Vision and Goals:** Remind yourself and your team of the bigger picture and the goals you're working towards. This reaffirmation helps to maintain focus and motivation, even in the face of challenges.
- **Adjust Your Strategy:** Based on the lessons learned. This might mean setting new milestones, exploring different approaches, or redefining goals to better align with current realities.
- **Celebrate Progress:** Recognize and celebrate each step forward, no matter how small. This recognition boosts morale and reinforces the mindset that setbacks are not the end but a part of the growth journey.

The Importance of Sticking With It and Being Strong

The ability to bounce back is the secret to overcoming challenges in life, and the key is to learn from your mistakes. Resilience gives leaders the courage to take on obstacles, grow from experience, and become stronger on the other side. It plays a complex role in this process, touching on all leadership facets.

Resilience is fundamental to effective leadership, particularly in the face of adversity. It's the force that propels you forward, transforming obstacles into clear pathways toward tremendous success. With flexibility, every setback becomes a setup for a powerful comeback, reinforcing the belief that challenges, no matter how daunting, are merely precursors to more extraordinary achievements.

9.4 RESILIENCE IN ACTION: LESSONS FROM SUCCESSFUL WOMEN LEADERS

In the tapestry of leadership, stories of women who have navigated through storms and emerged stronger provide a rich source of inspiration and wisdom. With their unique blend of tenacity and vision, these leaders demonstrate that resilience is about enduring, growing, and thriving in adversity.

Resilient Women Leaders: Their Stories

Women have paved new paths in the current state of leadership. From tech millionaires to social organizers, their leadership journeys are testaments to the power of resilience. They faced professional setbacks, personal challenges, and societal barriers, yet they pushed forward, driven by a belief in their vision and capabilities.

Moments of doubt, failure, and critique mark each leader's story. Yet, it was their response to these moments that defined their path. Some found resilience in their quiet determination to prove critics wrong, while others found it in their boldness to venture into uncharted territories despite the risks. These stories highlight a common thread —the refusal to be defined by setbacks and the courage to use them as catalysts for growth and change.

For instance, consider a tech entrepreneur who faced skepticism and rejection when pitching her groundbreaking idea. Each "no" fueled her drive to refine her pitch, broaden her network, and deepen her industry knowledge. Her persistence paid off in securing investment and launching a product that would revolutionize the market.

Another example is a social activist who saw her efforts dismissed and belittled and was often told that change was impossible. Instead of letting this deter her, she used it as motivation to forge stronger coalitions, harness the power of social media, and spread her cause to a global audience. Her resilience turned a seemingly impossible challenge into a movement that inspired people everywhere.

Lessons From Their Resilience

These stories, while unique, offer universal lessons on resilience that can guide any leader.

Applying the Approach

- **Persistence Pays Off:** Rejection and failure are not the end but a step in the journey. Persistence, coupled with the willingness to learn and adapt, can turn setbacks into success.
- **Vision Drives Resilience:** Holding a clear, compelling vision can be your anchor in turbulent times. It keeps the focus on the bigger picture and provides a sense of purpose that fuels perseverance.
- **Flexibility is Key:** Resilience is characterized by the ability to pivot and adapt strategies in response to setbacks. This ability ensures that challenges become opportunities for innovation and growth.

By neatly knitting together these threads of rapid recovery, successful women leaders teach us that learning to dance in the rain is just as crucial as surviving the storm. They serve as a reminder that what makes a leader great is not the lack of difficulties but rather the capacity to overcome them.

As we move forward, let's carry with us the understanding that resilience is a dynamic force we can cultivate and strengthen over time. It's about facing challenges with courage, gaining knowledge from each failure, and emerging unscathed, stronger, and wiser. This approach enriches our leadership journey and serves as a beacon for those we lead, inspiring them to navigate their challenges with grace and tenacity.

The Resilience Checklist

- Acknowledge your feelings in the face of setbacks, but don't let them steer the ship.
- Seek the lesson in every challenge. There's always something to learn.
- Set realistic, incremental goals to get back on track. Small wins build momentum.
- Lean on your support network. You don't have to face challenges alone.
- Celebrate your strength. Recognize and reward yourself and your team for bouncing back.

CHAPTER 10

5 WAYS TO FUTURE-PROOF YOUR CAREER IN THE AGE OF AI

"Learn to learn. Because what got you here won't get you there."

MARSHALL GOLDSMITH (EXECUTIVE COACH AND AUTHOR, 2007)

Women executives encounter new possibilities and threats in the dynamic business environment where artificial intelligence (AI) is increasingly important. When discussing leadership in the AI era, we can't help but bring up topics like the future of work, how technology and ethics interact, the value of continuous learning, and how leaders can benefit their businesses, workers, and the world. Technology strategists, business executives, and anyone curious about how AI will change leadership and organizational dynamics would find this interesting.

To keep your career solid and secure in the future, you must deliberately navigate and embrace these changes as a woman in a leadership position. Beyond the more obvious topics we have discussed in the book, know that diving deeper into practical methods of using technology in your leadership style and strategy for professional growth is vital. In our newer AI-driven business world (regardless of industry), the summaries below attempt to equip you with helpful insights and tactics to thrive now.

A commitment to lifelong learning is the cornerstone of career resilience in the digital age. As AI and automation change the nature of work, the demand for new skills and knowledge grows. Engaging in continuous professional development through formal education, online courses, or workshops is essential. Focus on both technical skills related to your field and emerging technologies and soft skills that are increasingly valuable in a tech-centric workplace.

During 2017 and 2018, I undertook a life-altering educational adventure, devoting myself to a sequence of in-depth classes focused on AI. Thanks to this challenging academic endeavor, I gained much information beyond the basics, significantly improving my comprehension of this cutting-edge technology. I learned about the details and importance of data, the Internet of Things (IOT), natural language generation, WEB3, and more.

Taking these classes was like diving headfirst into artificial intelligence; we covered everything from neural networks to machine learning algorithms. I understood the intricacies of AI and its possible effects on many businesses because they combined theoretical understanding and practical implementation.

The advantages of these classes, however, extended well beyond the classroom. In addition to bolstering my confidence, they gave me the tools I needed to thrive in the dynamic business world. I honed my skills in strategically applying AI concepts and coordinating technological solutions with business goals to fuel innovation and expansion.

These AI classes were the catalyst I needed to launch my career in the right direction, and I found a new passion. They helped me become more proficient in technology and gave me the tools I needed to think strategically, both of which are essential in today's fast-paced corporate environment.

Artificial intelligence's incorporation into business is happening now, not just in theory. This creates a double whammy for women in leadership positions: first, keeping up with technological changes; second, negotiating the subtleties of leadership roles frequently defined by long-standing conventions. The enormous opportunity to reimagine leadership and create a new paradigm at the intersection of technology and visionary leadership resides within this challenge. As we enter the age of artificial intelligence, let's explore ways women leaders might secure their jobs.

10.1 ADOPT A TECH-SAVVY MINDSET

If you have not already, adopting a tech-savvy mindset is non-negotiable to remain competitive in today's AI-driven world. This doesn't mean you need to become an expert in coding or machine learning, but having a foundational understanding of these technologies and how they impact your industry can be incredibly beneficial. Stay informed about the latest tech trends, and don't shy away from using new tools and platforms. This proactive approach will make you more adaptable and open new avenues for innovation in your work.

Being technologically adept is now essential, not a luxury, in this age of ubiquitous technology. The key is to train your brain to welcome novelty, be open to new ideas, and see technology's revolutionary potential. The key is to embrace change, adapt to a constantly changing digital environment, and use technology to your advantage for more efficiency, creativity, and productivity.

Applying the Approach

- **Tech-Enabled Problem Solving:** Cultivate the ability to approach challenges with a tech-savvy mindset. This involves thinking about how technology can solve complex problems, improve team efficiency, and enhance customer experiences. Bridging the gap between technical solutions and business goals is a valuable skill in a tech-driven corporate world.
- **Understanding the Ethical Implications of AI:** As AI becomes more integrated into business operations, ethical considerations around its use become increasingly important. Develop a deep understanding of AI's ethical implications, including bias, privacy, and accountability. Leading with a moral compass in deploying AI technologies ensures sustainable and responsible growth.

10.2 MASTER AI AND DATA LITERACY

Mastering AI and data literacy is increasingly becoming a cornerstone for effective leadership in the modern corporate environment. This necessity stems from the rapid integration of artificial intelligence and data analytics into various business operations, from strategic planning and decision-making to customer service and product development. For leaders, particularly women in leadership who are pioneering new paths in traditionally male-dominated sectors, comprehending, understanding, and leveraging these technologies is crucial.

Understanding AI and Data

The ability of a leader to use AI technologies and make data-driven decisions is becoming a determining factor in how effective they are in the digital age. Spend some time understanding the basic foundations of data analytics, machine learning, and artificial intelligence. Online tools, books, and courses can provide much-needed information. In turn, this puts you in a position to lead your team through technological changes and make well-informed judgments as a forward-thinking leader.

Driving Digital Transformation

Leaders must identify these opportunities and champion adopting and integrating AI into their organization's culture and processes. This involves advocating for necessary investments in technology and facilitating training and development for their team.

Women in positions of power must continue to become data literate and experts in artificial intelligence to stay abreast of technical developments and pave the way for transformational leadership that uses AI to drive innovation, efficiency, and ethical practices. By adopting data literacy and artificial intelligence, leaders can motivate their teams to do the same, succeed in an AI-driven world, and negotiate the digital age's intricacies. Executives, through this ongoing education and strategic planning process, position themselves to become futuristic visionaries capable of shaping their industries' futures through technology.

10.3 ETHICAL CONSIDERATIONS IN AI-AUGMENTED DECISION MAKING

In today's new technological developments, integrating Artificial Intelligence into decision-making processes marks a pivotal evolution, enhancing productivity and modernization. However, this integration brings the critical importance of ethical considerations to the forefront. As we navigate this juncture, it becomes paramount for technical leaders to ensure that AI systems are designed and implemented with a deep commitment to ethical principles.

Firstly, accountability and transparency stand at the core of ethical AI use. Technical leaders must advocate for systems that explain their decisions in understandable terms. This transparency cultivates trust among stakeholders and guarantees the identification and correction of any biases or errors in the AI's decision-making process. Accountability mechanisms should be in place to attribute responsibility for the decisions made by AI systems, ensuring that there are human oversight and intervention capabilities.

Furthermore, fairness and bias mitigation are essential. AI systems learn from vast datasets, which can contain implicit human biases. Leaders are responsible for implementing rigorous bias detection and mitigation strategies. This involves diverse and inclusive data collection, continuous monitoring for biased outcomes, and adjusting algorithms accordingly. Ensuring fairness in AI's decisions helps prevent discrimination and promotes equity, which is crucial in maintaining the social license to operate.

Privacy protection also emerges as a significant ethical concern. AI systems often process sensitive personal information; thus, safeguarding this data against unauthorized access or misuse is imperative. Leaders should champion data protection practices that exceed mere compliance, embedding privacy by design into AI systems. This entails handling data with respect, obtaining consent when required, and utilizing it solely for its intended ethical purposes.

We cannot overstate the ethical dimensions of AI's use as it becomes increasingly embedded in corporate decision-making. Leaders must be the vanguards of ethical AI, championing accountability, fairness, and privacy. By making this commitment, we can harness AI's transformative power in an innovative manner that aligns with the highest ethical standards, ensuring that technology serves the needs of all involved.

10.4 DRIVE CHANGE CREATIVELY

Encourage a culture where change and innovation are valued, and failure is seen as a step towards progress. This involves championing initiatives that explore new technologies, including AI, and their application in your industry. By fostering an environment that supports experimentation and learning, you pave the way for your organization to remain competitive and adaptive.

Participate actively in spearheading your company's digital transformation efforts. This includes ensuring your team has access to the resources they need, advocating for the adoption of new technology, and using digital tools to streamline operations. How quickly and effectively digital integration takes place depends on your openness to embrace change.

10.5 BOOSTING RESILIENCE AND VERSATILITY FOR TODAY'S TECHNOLOGICALLY ADVANCED TIME

Being open to new situations and challenges is more important than ever. AI and automation are transforming traditional positions and creating new ones, often requiring professionals to step out of their comfort zones. Cultivating a mindset that views change as an opportunity rather than a threat will enable you to navigate career transitions more smoothly. Be open to acquiring new skills and taking on different responsibilities as your job evolves alongside technological advancements.

The pace of technological innovation means that business models, processes, and strategies are constantly evolving. Adaptable and flexible leaders can quickly integrate new technologies, like AI, into their operations, gaining a competitive edge and driving innovation.

The modern business environment is characterized by volatility and uncertainty. Flexible leaders can pivot strategies in response to unexpected challenges, such as market shifts or global events, ensuring organizational resilience.

In an age where AI and digital transformation are reshaping the corporate world, extensive learning is an indispensable quality for leaders. By fostering these skills, women leaders can navigate the complexities of technological advancement and confidently lead their organizations through periods of change.

10.6 A BREAKTHROUGH IN LEADERSHIP

Influential leaders' abilities and characteristics must change along with the fabric of leadership. Future leaders need to be tech-savvy, meaning they need to know the newest technologies and how to use them. It's time to get ready, not just by honing your abilities but also by expanding your horizons.

Introspection is one of many steps on the trip. Consider your past experiences, the knowledge you gained, and how they influenced your leadership. Reflect on your motivations and fundamental beliefs. How do they fit into this new position? Knowing your talents and potential growth areas lays the groundwork for authentic leadership, self-assurance, and moral rectitude. It all comes down to understanding your leadership identity and your future goals.

Another reminder! No leader stands alone. Continue cultivating a network of tech-savvy mentors, peers, and sponsors who can offer guidance and support. These relationships can be a source of invaluable insights and encouragement, helping you navigate the intricacies of your position.

By actively developing these skills and qualities, leaders equip themselves to navigate the challenges of tomorrow, leading with insight and innovation. Preparing for your next leadership role is an ongoing process that requires dedication, self-awareness, and a proactive approach to personal and professional development. By focusing on these strategies, you can build a solid foundation for successful leadership and make a positive impact in your future jobs. Remember, the leadership journey is as much about developing others as it is about personal growth.

10.7 LEADING IN A WORLD THAT IS EVER-CHANGING

Change is the only constant in the corporate world. In this environment, leaders embrace change not as a threat but as a chance for learning and development. This calls for a versatile approach to thought and action, an openness to shift plans when presented with new data, and the fortitude to endure obstacles while relentlessly pressing on. I know it is a challenging request, and if you can embrace the changes, you will come out on top. I assure you!

Leading organizations through a transition that aligns with changing consumer needs, social norms, and technological breakthroughs is another aspect of effective leadership in a changing environment—foreseeing and reacting to external forces, whether political, social, environmental, or economic, is essential for effective leadership. It also demands having a thorough awareness of the global environment. Influential leaders can anticipate several scenarios, plan for them, and prepare their companies to change course when needed. This strategic foresight guarantees the business will stay ahead of the curve with proactive rather than reactive measures.

In navigating the changing leadership landscape, the most influential leaders anticipate and adapt to change and inspire and empower others to do the same. They understand that in a world of constant flux, the ability to lead through change is not just a skill but a true superpower.

CHAPTER 11

WHAT LIES AHEAD FOR WOMEN IN EXECUTIVE ROLES

As discussed throughout the book, there is a new era of women in leadership positions, and it is not just around the corner; it is bursting forth like the sun, illuminating the world and putting the old ways of doing things in their dust. The current epoch is revolutionizing global leadership by being dynamic through a loud and unapologetic takeover rather than a subtle elevation to power.

11.1 THE CONTINUED RISE OF WOMEN IN LEADERSHIP

For decades, the leadership environment resembled a rough mountain range with towering peaks that many found unattainable. However, the narrative has been quickly changing. Today, we're witnessing an increasing number of women scaling these heights, not just reaching the summit but also paving new paths. As women, we bring unique strengths to this landscape, blending intuition with resilience to foster environments where creativity and growth flourish. Our approach to leadership is not about wielding power but about empowering others.

The rise of women in the leadership ranks across sectors—from technology and finance to healthcare and education—is not just a trend. A combination of factors fuels this shift: advocacy for gender equality, organizational policies promoting diversity and inclusion, and a growing recognition of women's unique perspectives and skills in leadership positions. As women, our contribution to this new era of leadership extends beyond our immediate circles; it has the power to transform societies. By leading with empathy, championing diversity, creating safe spaces, and advocating for inclusivity, we create more equitable workplaces and contribute to a more just world. The dawn of this new era is our call to action, inviting us to lead boldly, passionately, and with a profound sense of purpose.

Looking ahead, the trajectory for women in leadership and executive positions is promising and pivotal. The next decade will likely see an acceleration of this shift, with more women stepping into more prominent roles and shaping the future of their organizations. The challenge now is not just about breaking through the glass ceiling but about ensuring that once through, women will lead in a way that's authentic to them without having to conform to outdated leadership models.

This trajectory is not just a possibility; it's within your reach. Both individuals and organizations must take action. It calls for continued advocacy for gender equality, policies that support work-life integration, and a commitment to cultivating a diverse and inclusive leadership pipeline.

Women leaders have a unique value that combines the complexities of caring leadership with the ability to see the big picture. Their approach often embodies strength and sensitivity, enabling them to navigate complex challenges with a unique perspective. This dual capability enhances team dynamics, drives performance, nurtures innovation, and strengthens stakeholder relationships.

From an economic perspective, empowering women in the work-place contributes to economic growth. Increasing women's participation in leadership has been shown to boost bottom-line numbers, demonstrating not just a moral or ethical imperative for gender equality but a solid economic one.

11.2 SEVEN STRATEGIES FOR SUCCESS AS ASPIRING EXECUTIVES

1. Victory in the Small Battles

- Successful women savor the thrill of challenge and competition, cherishing even minor victories. These triumphs bolster confidence and enhance motivation, setting the stage for more considerable successes.

2. An Open Mind

- Openness to diverse perspectives is a hallmark of successful leadership. Successful women leaders value empathy and understanding, enriching their worldviews and uncovering opportunities for growth in every interaction.

3. Unwavering Confidence

- A critical attribute is the courage to act on one's ideas, undeterred by the prospect of failure. For successful women, setbacks are not reflections of inadequacy but invaluable learning experiences.

4. Composure Under Pressure

- Mastery over one's emotions, especially in tumultuous situations, ensures steady leadership. Successful women maintain their poise, know that time brings change, and are adaptable, which is crucial to staying in control.

5. Diverse Associations

- Exposure to contrasting perspectives fuels innovation. Successful women leaders foster creativity and build robust, dynamic teams by engaging with individuals who challenge and complement their thinking.

6. Grounded Dreamers

- While their aspirations may reach the skies, successful women leaders remain firmly grounded in reality. Actionable steps toward lofty goals, no matter how incremental, mark their journey.

7. Fearlessness

- These leaders confront fear and transform it into a catalyst for action. Recognizing fear as a construct of the mind, they face it head-on, relishing the thrill of overcoming it.

By adopting these strategies, female executives in corporate companies can navigate the path to leadership with confidence and grace.

11.3 CRAFTING THE FUTURE OF WORK

In today's rapidly evolving business environment, female leaders are at the forefront of driving transformation. Their commitment to promoting a corporate culture that values what we have discussed in this book is not merely ideological but eminently practical.

In this transformative age, women's leadership is indispensable. Their contributions enhance the present and define the future of work. Women's leadership will drive a more inclusive, innovative, and resilient future as the corporate world evolves.

It is essential to be aware of and actively participate in the ever-changing dynamics of corporate leadership. We invite every prospective leader to contribute to the transformative shift of women assuming leadership positions.

Embracing Your Full Potential—YOU Got This!

Unlocking your leadership potential begins with self-recognition. It's about acknowledging your distinctive strengths, experiences, and perspectives that you bring to the table. Recognizing your potential is the first step in a series of deliberate actions to refine and deploy your leadership skills.

We have discussed all the steps you must take to succeed in this book. Remember to continue seeking challenges outside your comfort zone, as this is where growth happens. Volunteer for new projects and apply your talents in novel ways.

The journey is unique to everyone, filled with challenges that test your limits and moments of clarity that reveal your true strength.

Your road towards realizing your potential is uniquely yours, yet it contributes to the collective progress of women. By embracing your unique power, you will inspire other women to do the same, creating a ripple effect that enriches this landscape.

11.4 PREPARING FOR THE LEADERSHIP CHALLENGES OF TOMORROW

The world of leadership is broad, dynamic, and even surprising, much like the ocean. To navigate this vast area, one must have unwavering grit, skill, vision, flexibility, and a thorough comprehension of the waves of change ahead.

As a leader, you are constantly facing challenges. Keeping up with the ever-changing relationship between technological advancement, social and economic changes, and environmental factors is crucial for leaders who want to foresee the difficulties they may face in the future. Leaders must be ready to deal with the increasing demands for environmentally and socially responsible business practices, the ethical dilemmas posed by data privacy and artificial intelligence, and the complexity of our increasingly linked world. To have this vision, one must keep up with the latest technological developments and develop a profound understanding and compassion for today's multicultural and global workforce's wide range of beliefs and perspectives.

Maintaining team cohesiveness, cultivating a robust organizational culture, and ensuring productivity and well-being across dispersed teams are all made more difficult by the proliferation of remote and hybrid work arrangements. For leaders to thrive in a dynamic and unpredictable environment, they need to see the big picture, be flexible, and have high emotional intelligence. Only then will they be able to inspire confidence, propel innovation, and lead with honesty.

Remember to stay ahead and be proactive in anticipating challenges, which is crucial.

Takeaways

- Keeping abreast of technological trends and their potential impact on business and society.
- Engaging with experts and thought leaders on sustainability to integrate eco-friendly practices into business models.
- Listening to and learning from diverse voices within and outside the organization to build a more inclusive corporate culture.

Adopting a forward-thinking mindset enables leaders to not just react to challenges as they arise but to anticipate them, preparing strategies that turn potential obstacles into opportunities for growth and innovation.

11.5 BUILDING LEADERS OF TOMORROW

Today's trailblazers stand upon a precipice in the grand theater of leadership, gazing ahead at an emerging generation of fierce, ambitious women ready to take the world by storm. These upcoming professionals aren't mere spectators; they are the masterminds, the innovators, and the game-changers waiting in the wings, their potential simmering just beneath the surface, ready to erupt.

We can wield the power to pass the baton and craft the very race that lies ahead. It's a thrilling challenge, a spicy blend of mentorship, encouragement, and equitable opportunities, concocted to empower these female dynamos and provoke their latent ability.

The world is ready for a paradigm shift, ready to tear down the archaic walls of gender bias and welcome a new era of balanced leadership. Are you, as a leader, prepared to fan the flame of progress and stoke the fires of ambition in these rising stars?

The question is more than how you can support these upcoming female professionals. Still, how you can conspire with them, stand shoulder to shoulder with them in the face of adversity, and rise together.

What part do you play? Act as an ally, a mentor, and a catalyst. Today's leaders hold the key to redefining many of our beliefs. Taste the spice, embrace the heat, and let's light the world on fire together.

An exciting new era is dawning in the business world, and it will be characterized by a diverse and inclusive chorus of voices demanding equality, empowerment, and inclusion. Among these voices is a chorus of exceptionally talented women who are influential, audacious, and identifiable. We can enhance the clarity of their music, but this is the booming symphony of today, not the voices of tomorrow, and they are ready to completely transform the corporate language.

Create initiatives to empower all women with the skills, confidence, and knowledge necessary to navigate the corporate labyrinth. These initiatives are springboards, propelling women into the stratospheres of leadership with a potent blend of training, networking, and hands-on experience. Lay the groundwork for a culture of inclusivity, where every voice is heard, every talent recognized, and every woman is allowed to rise.

Opening doors for young women entering the workforce to assume leadership positions is like illuminating a hidden road. Our responsibility is to support and provide environments where people may lead initiatives, steer conversations, or control decision-making. Every leadership experience strengthens their commitment, boosts their self-assurance, and prepares them for challenges. It's about encouraging them to cross the barrier with confidence in their talents and courage, not just in opening doors but also in creating new gates.

Women leaders are fundamentally reshaping the corporate landscape through their visionary approach to organizational transformation, commitment to building inclusive leadership pipelines, and strategic use of technology for inclusion. Their efforts are about achieving excellence within their respective organizations and contributing to a broader societal change toward greater inclusivity, equity, and sustainability. As we move forward, the job of women in leadership positions will undoubtedly continue to be pivotal in driving progress and innovation in the corporate world and beyond.

Your function in shaping the future of leadership is critical. By embracing your leadership potential, advocating for women in leadership, and actively contributing to the leadership narrative, you create a future where leadership is defined by capability, innovation, and inclusivity. This journey has challenges but promises a more equitable, dynamic, and successful corporate world. Your contribution to this landscape is not just valuable; it's essential.

CONCLUSION

IGNITING CHANGE: A RALLYING CRY FOR CONTINUED PROGRESS

You've just sprinted through the final lap of what I hope has been an exhilarating journey from the entry lines to the peaks of excellence in leadership. If you're feeling a bit winded, that's okay. Consider this: every challenge you faced, every obstacle you overcame, didn't just happen. They were the essential ingredients in the recipe for your growth. Think of it as the ultimate workout for your leadership muscles, with each hurdle making you stronger and more resilient. And just like the most rewarding hikes lead to the best views, the journey you've embarked on leads to a form of leadership that's not just effective but transformative. Greatness never comes easy, but oh, is it worth the climb?

In our modern world, where every headline seems to herald new challenges, igniting change isn't just a noble idea; it's a necessary call to action for all of us. Recognizing that we need more than the status quo and that pursuing progress is an endless journey is crucial.

Do you remember when we started this adventure? As we stood at the threshold, you might have been unsure of our direction. Now, look at you, armed with the proper toolbox, insights, strategies, and, most importantly, the confidence to carve your path with influence in the leadership landscape. It's been quite the ride!

While we redefine leadership now, we've unpacked the dynamite of women's leadership, haven't we? From embracing empathy and resilience to championing diversity and innovation, you've seen how these aren't just buzzwords but the very pillars that can uphold and propel organizations toward success. Women like us don't just lead; we transform!

At its core, igniting change is about the courage to confront the uncomfortable, to challenge the norms that no longer serve us, and to ask the hard questions about who we are and who we want to be, both as individuals and as a society. It's about seeing beyond the immediate horizon and daring to imagine a better future.

Most Important Points to Remember From the Book

- **Innovative Leadership Models:** Challenge traditional leadership models by experimenting with approaches that emphasize collaboration, empathy, and inclusivity. Your leadership model can serve as a blueprint for others, showcasing the effectiveness of diverse leadership styles.
- **Cultivating Diverse Teams:** Make diversity a cornerstone of your leadership. Assemble teams that reflect a broad spectrum of backgrounds, experiences, and perspectives. This diversity enriches the team's creativity and problem-solving abilities and mirrors the diverse world we navigate.
- **Leading with Authenticity:** In a world often dominated by archaic leadership stereotypes, your authenticity is a refreshing change. Lead in a way true to your values,

experiences, and vision. Authentic leadership inspires trust, loyalty, and engagement among your team.

Your Call-to-Action

Lead, Advocate, and Inspire: What's next? It's showtime. It's your turn to take the stage and lead with the wisdom and flair you possess. But don't stop there. Advocate for those coming up behind you. Be the mentor you wish you had. And most of all, inspiring. Light up with your successes and grace in navigating all your experiences.

Talk about the importance of being a beacon of hope and encouragement. Urge women leaders to showcase their achievements and the positive impact of their leadership. Highlight how showcasing leadership can ignite passion and ambition in others.

Final Thoughts

This isn't a "goodbye." It's a 'see you at the summit.' Your leadership journey is an ever-evolving story. Keep learning, stay curious, and never doubt your power to effect change. Join networks, seek out challenges, and remember, I'm cheering for you every step of the way.

Ultimately, it matters more than just the titles and honors we accumulate. It concerns the lives we affect, the surroundings we improve, and the legacy we leave behind. What's going to be yours? What unique combination of abilities, interests, and life experiences will you employ to make a lasting impression on the world?

I've witnessed firsthand in my career the transformative power of leading with authenticity and vision through the trials of technology and hurdles in leadership. Like my two corgis, renowned not for their size but for their heart and spirit, I've learned that it's not the scale of your role but the magnitude of your impact that truly defines leadership excellence.

As our conversation ends in our warm and cozy café and we step back into the hustle and bustle of the world outside, let's carry the resolve to ignite change in our corners of the universe. Let this be our rallying cry, a testament to our belief in the possibility of a better tomorrow.

So here's to you, to us, and to the incredible journey ahead. Let's make it legendary.

SHARE IT WITH OTHERS!
REVIEW REQUEST

The mission is to create a world where women feel empowered to achieve higher levels.

This is where you come in. Most people judge a book by its cover (and it is Reviews). So, here's my ask to you, leaders and achievers in business!

Please help those new and aspiring leaders by leaving an honest review.

Scan the QR code with your smartphone camera below to leave your review:

Or Use the Link:
https://www.amazon.com/Womens-Success-Corporate-Leadership-Inspiration/dp/B0D4R62436/

With heartfelt thanks,

René Clayton

REFERENCES

Advisor, W. (2023, December 1). *Examining CEO Jane Fraser's Strategic Vision for Citigroup.* The Wealth Advisor. https://www.thewealthadvisor.com/article/examining-ceo-jane-frasers-strategic-vision-citigroup

Birwal, K. (n.d.). *Practical strategies for continuous leadership development.* LinkedIn. https://www.linkedin.com/pulse/effective-strategies-continuous-leadership-kuldeep-birwal

Bourke, J., & Dillon, B. (2019, March 29). Why inclusive leaders are suitable for organizations, and how to become one. Harvard Business Review. https://hbr.org/2019/03/why-inclusive-leaders-are-good-for-organizations-and-how-to-become-one

Chief's Study Finds 80% of Women Leaders Use Networking to Drive Career Success. (2023, July 19). Business Wire. https://www.businesswire.com/news/home/20230719423838/en/Chief%E2%80%99s-Study-Finds-80-of-Women-Leaders-Use-Networking-to-Drive-Career-Success

D. (2022, February 26). *The Art of Persuasion in Leadership.* Eagle's Flight. https://www.eaglesflight.com/resource/the-art-of-persuasion-in-leadership/

D., & D. (2023, August 8). *Resilient leadership: Easy steps to navigate the working life pressure.* IMD Business School for Management and Leadership Courses. https://www.imd.org/research-knowledge/articles/resilient-leadership-navigating-the-pressures-of-modern-working-life/

Embracing Self-Acceptance to Break Free from the Chains of Self-Doubt. (2023, APril 20) Rick Woman Magazine. https://richwoman.co/embracing-self-acceptance-to-break-free-from-the-chains-of-self-doubt/

Experts, D. (2023, January 15). *2021 Benchmark Report for Revenue Leaders.* DealHub. https://dealhub.io/blog/revenue-operations/2021-benchmark-report-for-revenue-leaders/

Forbes Business Council. (2023, May 1). *Building Agile teams: 13 tips to foster employee adaptability.* Forbes. https://www.forbes.com/sites/forbesbusinesscouncil/2023/05/01/building-agile-teams-13-tips-to-foster-employee-adaptability/

Forbes Coaches Council. (2023, February 2). *How to build and maintain professional relationships.* Forbes. https://www.forbes.com/sites/forbescoachescouncil/2023/02/02/how-to-build-and-maintain-professional-relationships/

Harms, P. D., & Credé, M. (2023). Emotional Intelligence and Transformational Leadership. *Journal of Managerial Psychology, 38*(7), 1–15. https://www.ncbi.nlm.nih.gov/pmc/articles/PMC9680507/

Harvard Business School Online. (n.d.). *Resilient Leadership: 4 Ways to Build Resilience.* HBS Online. https://online.hbs.edu/blog/post/resilient-leadership

Ho, L. (2023, August 16). *The Ultimate Guide to Prioritizing Your Work And Life.* Lifehack. https://www.lifehack.org/810807/prioritizing-work-and-life

Hyken, S. (2018, February 25). *A $600 billion employee engagement problem solved: Empathy.* Forbes. https://www.forbes.com/sites/shephyken/2018/02/25/a-600-billion-employee-engagement-problem-solved-empathy/

Ibarra, H., & Hunter, M. L. (2007, January). *How leaders create and use networks.* Harvard Business Review. https://hbr.org/2007/01/how-leaders-create-and-use-networks

Johnson, B., & Lee, C. (2022). *What leaders get wrong about resilience.* Harvard Business Review. https://www.hbr.org

Kim, L. (2019). The visionary leadership needed to power the next wave of global innovation. *Leadership Quarterly, 10*(4), 158–172

Koirala, S. (2023, July 3). *Turning Setbacks into Comebacks: Stories of Resilience and Triumph.* Medium. https://medium.com/@sristikoirala7/turning-setbacks-into-comebacks-stories-of-resilience-and-triumph-476dbcc2f929

Lifelong Learner: How Continuous Learning Benefits Leaders. (n.d.). Maven. https://maven.com/articles/lifelong-learner

Malik, R. (2023, July 17). *Distinct Roles of Allies and Advocates: Laying the Foundation for an Inclusive Work Environment.* LinkeIin. https://www.linkedin.com/pulse/distinct-roles-allies-advocates-laying-foundation-rubina-malik-ph-d-

Malin, A. (2023, February 1). *The Future of Women's Leadership: an Expert Guide to How We Lead in 2023.* AllBright. https://www.allbrightcollective.com/edit/articles/the-future-of-womens-leadership-an-expert-guide-to-how-we-lead-in-2023

Mary Barra Leadership: Analysis & Impact. (n.d.). Vaia. https://www.hellovaia.com/explanations/business-studies/business-case-studies/mary-barra-leadership-style/

Maximizing Sales Conversions with Optimized Lead Generation. (2023, May 30). Famous Gold State. https://famousgoldstate.com/26068-maximizing-sales-conversions-with-optimized-lead-generation-45/

Miller, H. L. (2022, March 10). *Whitney Wolfe Herd: Standing Out in a Saturated Market.* Leaders.com. https://leaders.com/articles/leadership/whitney-wolfe-herd/

Moyer, L. (2024, March 21). *Jane Fraser.* Barrons. https://www.barrons.com/articles/barrons-100-most-influential-women-in-u-s-finance-jane-fraser-c6d71ee4

National Geographic Society. (2023, October 19). *Women of NASA.* National Geographic Education. https://education.nationalgeographic.org/resource/women-nasa/

Niver, L. (2020, August 9). *Is Talking Through Technology Making You More Human? with Rana el Kaliouby.* Thrive Global. https://community.thriveglobal.com/is-talking-through-technology-making-you-more-human-with-rana-el-kaliouby/

Nordqvist, C. (2023, August 29). *Employee Monitoring in a Remote Work*

Environment: Finding the Right Balance. Market Business News. https://market businessnews.com/employee-monitoring-in-a-remote-work-environment-finding-the-right-balance/345205/

Rhodes, M. G. (2021, December 14). *Women Who Successfully Balance Leadership, Family and Wellbeing Have These 3 Things in Common.* Entrepreneur. https://www.entrepreneur.com/leadership/women-who-successfully-balance-leadership-family-and/397604

Scott, M. (2023, June) *How to be strong and courageous.* Lifestyle & Culture - Crossmap Communities - Christian Forums. https://communities.crossmap.com/t/how-to-be-strong-and-courageous/4480

Seven visionary women who are passionate about leadership. (n.d.). Fast Company. https://board.fastcompany.com/blog/visionary-women-passionate-about-leadership

Staff, B. (2024, February 26). *Employees Who Challenge The Status Quo: How They Make A Difference?* Business Management Blog. https://businessmanagement blog.com/challenge-the-status-quo/

T. (2023, September 19). *The Importance of Credibility in Leadership.* Triple Crown Leadership. https://triplecrownleadership.com/the-importance-of-credibility-in-leadership/

The Benefits of Strengths-based Leadership. (2021, April 19). Training Industry. https://trainingindustry.com/articles/leadership/the-benefits-of-strengths-based-leadership/

The Feminine Advantage: 4 Unique Qualities Women Bring to the Workplace. (n.d.). Worldwide Learn. https://www.worldwidelearn.com/articles/4-unique-qualities-women-bring-to-the-workplace/

The Top 10 Influential Women in Leadership for 2023. (2023). The National Society of Leadership and Success. https://www.nsls.org/blog/the-top-10-influential-women-in-leadership-for-2023

Transformation starts with agile leadership. (n.d.). McKinsey & Company. https://www.mckinsey.com/capabilities/people-and-organizational-performance/our-insights/leading-agile-transformation-the-new-capabilities-leaders-need-to-build-21st-century-organizations

Treasure, J. (n.d.). *How to speak so that people want to listen.* TED Talks. https://www.ted.com/talks/julian_treasure_how_to_speak_so_that_people_want_to_listen

13 of the most powerful women in business. (2023, June). Husson University. https://www.husson.edu/online/blog/2023/06/powerful-women-in-business

What are some effective strategies for managing stress and anxiety during JEE preparation? (2023, January 10). Exprto | India's Largest Mentorship Community. https://ask.exprto.com/t/what-are-some-effective-strategies-for-managing-stress-and-anxiety-during-jee-preparation/9071

Williams, G. (2023, July 25). *Life Path Number 8: Mastering the Journey of Leadership and Success.* MindEasy. https://mindeasy.com/life-path-number-8/

Women in the Workplace 2023 report. (2023). McKinsey & Company. https://www.
mckinsey.com/featured-insights/diversity-and-inclusion/women-in-the-workplace

World's Visionary Women Leaders Making an Impact in 2023. (2023, December).
World's Leaders. https://worldsleaders.com/worlds-visionary-women-leaders-
making-an-impact-in-2023-dec23/